TRUE JU

THE DIVINE FAMILY: A TRUE JOURNEY INTO BIBLICAL POLYGYNY

- From Identity To Culture, A Modern Approach To Living As Our Ancient Hebraic Family

To all of my brothers and sisters who love the Truth. May you continue to be bold and intentional. To the courageous souls who embrace the path less traveled, may you find strength in your convictions.

Contents

Preface

The Divine Family: A True Journey into Biblical Polygyny is a unique and insightful resource for individuals and families exploring the idea of polygyny as it relates to the Bible. The book provides a historical and biblical perspective on polygyny, as well as a practical guide for those interested in building an expanded family strategy that works.

The author provides a balanced and thorough analysis of the subject matter, citing numerous examples from the Bible and other historical sources. The book also offers guidance on how to navigate the challenges of polygyny, such as jealousy, communication, and financial management.

One of the key benefits of this book is its focus on practicality. The author provides a step-by-step guide to building an expanded family strategy that works, including tips on how to find and court potential wives, how to manage household finances, and how to establish healthy communication practices within the family.

Whether you are a novice or an experienced leader, *The Divine Family: A True Journey into Biblical Polygyny* offers valuable insights and practical know-how for those exploring the concept of polygyny. With its balanced and thorough analysis of the subject matter, and its practical guidance on building an expanded family strategy that works, this book is an essential resource for anyone interested in this fascinating and complex topic.

Introduction - Papa's Perception

"Polygyny, conducted in truth, is a sacrifice in and of itself. To establish a healthy and equitable polygynous unit, the man and women involved must all forfeit many selfish aspects of who they are."
  - **True Ju, Papa's Perception**

Popularity In Polygyny

As the return to traditional living has become more relevant in recent years, it is only during the past couple of years that we see an influx of polygynous unions taking place.

What I have personally noticed is an attempt to reconnect with Ancestral practices, usually with an overwhelming emphasis on spirituality.

Once an individual has begun the process of identifying who their particular ancestors and ancestresses are, they will more than likely be led to observe very specific practices based upon the direct lineages they belong to; primarily the maternal and paternal lineages being the ones identified with the most.

Due to this reality, the process of reconnecting with lost traditional practices and ways of living can take some time to get fully acclimated with.

One of the reasons a polygynous lifestyle is so alluring to many who seek the ways of old is because many of the ancestral traditions practiced on earth, beginning in ancient times, including the family structure founded in polygyny.

There seems to be a natural progression, or inclination, towards fully embracing traditional ancestral cultural elements, almost an innate feeling to return to a time when life appeared to be simpler.

The issue however is that modern men and women do not live in the days of old. We instead live during the social media era, pocket computers, and a growing detachment from all things organic, natural, and righteous within the eyes of the majority of the "Old Gods".

We now live in a time where what was once seen as correct and good, is now seen as aloof and bad.

When one seeks to chastise or even punish their child for a wrong committed by that child, the parent is oftentimes ostracized by society and others for seeking to exact the very punishment the offense requires from the parent, which is one of the reasons many have sought to return to a lifestyle of polygyny.

The communal aspects of Polygyny are usually one of the first realizations made by honest practitioners of the very ancient family structure.

As people have sought to return to a lifestyle of polygyny, some seek and crave the attention the lifestyle seems to attract.

Many of the most successful modern-day practitioners of polygyny do not broadcast that they practice or promote the lifestyle.

The rationalization behind this decision is immense.

For starters, we are living during a time when people seek to magnify anything that removes focus from off of themselves. Polygyny provides the perfect fuel and fodder for those bored, and idle individuals who love to stir controversy.

Even though polygyny is a righteous family structure, and based on positive communal growth, we do live in modern times, in a region of the world where monogamy was introduced as part of an act of war on the indigenous populations living during those early periods of European invasion and conquest; this is a reality that we must grasp if we are to move forward with the polygynous lifestyle in full confidence.

As active practitioners of polygyny, it is detrimental that we inner-stand the magnitude and psychological connotations behind introducing and forcing a certain marital system on people who always chose the best form of marriage for themselves, based upon their own needs, as well as those of the village or community they were members of.

The reasons for seeking validation within polygyny are immense, as each man who chooses to practice polygyny is unique, and by extension, so are his wives and children.

Many men first seek the validation of their God, their Holy Books, their ancestors and ancestresses, and any elders who may have advice to give on the subject. These are all honorable and admirable resources to rely upon when seeking to establish the traditions of old, in any sector of traditional thought and practice.

Many of these individuals seek to learn in a privatized manner, leading their family as carefully as possible while they learn and adopt the methods most beneficial to their particular family construct.

There's a saying that "any publicity is good publicity". However, within the confines of polygyny, this saying may not be true.

As the advent of social media appears to be at its climax in the year 2020, some seek to be validated in polygyny by their peers, as well as peer groups, whom they frequently joined.

These particular individuals, although living within many of the original tenets of polygyny, don't necessarily seek to remain out of the spotlight the lifestyle attracts.

Instead, these people have begun to leverage the attention in an attempt to transmute the negativity often associated with modern-day polygyny, to the chagrin of some, and the enjoyment of others.

From uploaded videos and posts on social media to private courses available online, the ones who've made a career out of teaching the tenets of polygyny have had their struggles, primarily the struggle of the decision to open up and share intimate details about their personal experiences within the lifestyle.

It is not easy for anyone to open up and share intimate information such as how they operate their home daily, all the while maintaining a marital structure perceived as taboo by the majority of Western society.

While it is not easy to open up and share intimate details about one's private life, it is of utmost importance to utilize a sense of discernment before inviting different sorts of energy into your home, personal space, and family structure.

Some have enjoyed and sought after the popularity of polygyny, over the proper practice of polygyny, to which they and their families have suffered greatly.

Many of these individuals have later gone on to regret and indemnify polygyny as an unviable familial structure, condemning the practice due to personal decisions that were not founded with the proper intent.

If this book is to be of any value, it is important to identify the psychology behind the reasons for many of the decisions made concerning a polygynous lifestyle. Attempting to identify every reason may, however, prove to be more cumbersome than rational.

Let us list a few of the reasons then.

In this way, we can begin to get the proverbial ball rolling and identify which reasons are healthy and which reasons may be more detrimental than helpful, when choosing and committing to a lifestyle of polygyny.

Unhealthy reasons -

- Attention seeking
- Personal popularity contest
- Financial greed
- Secularity
- Selfishness
- Controlling or domineering

Healthy reasons -

- Unity in Community
- Provide sound and righteous covering for the women of your people.
- Extended family structure
- Increased responsibility
- Ability to leverage the expertise of the family once matured
- Ability to grow the family economy quicker

Listed here, are but a few of the more common reasons, both healthy and unhealthy, which serve as impetus to participate in a polygynous union.

You'll do well in noticing that many of the unhealthy reasons listed are based on a one-sided, clouded perspective of what it means to function within a polygynous family construct, while the healthy reasons listed are based on a more nurturing and inclusive family paradigm.

It is also important to take note that the reasons listed above are given for example as being initiated by the man or husband, and not the first or subsequent wives.

The Balancing Act of Masculine Energy vs. The Carefulness of Naivety

Approaching Consummation With The Sensitivity Of Virginity

The initial act of consummation between my subsequent wife and I was somewhat mysterious in that we'd never engaged in any promiscuous activity while learning about one another before we joined in marriage.

We decided early on that we should institute the best practices known to us at the time, and that it would be wise not to engage in any actions that would come across as overtly sexual. The reason for this decision was purely predicated upon the desire to establish a relationship that wasn't based upon sexual desire or behavior, and more so based upon the spiritual aspects of a genuine union between man and woman. The sexual aspect of the relationship being obvious, we felt no need to expound upon it before making our union official through the signing of the marital contract, agreement with our family bylaws, and finally, physical consummation between the two of us.

The act of consummation between a husband and his new wife is a must in adjoining the physical aspect of the relationship with the spiritual aspect that has been previously established when both parties identified the viability of the relationship, to begin with.

However, if the husband has been married to his first wife for any extended period, he may be reluctant in moving forward with the physical aspect of consummation, even though he is aware of this requirement, and even though he may have a genuine sexual attraction to his second wife. He will find it difficult to move forward sexually if he consciously considers his first wife's potential feelings in hearing the news of his consummation to a second wife.

The husband is correct in his feelings and it is a great and divine opportunity for the second wife to be comforting and gentle in her response to him, even though she has patiently waited for that moment, and holds no subconscious or negatively conscious feelings towards her husband's first marriage.

What needs to be recognized is that the entire experience will be new, and have its nuances that all who participate must learn to deal with healthily.

Patience and transparent communication are key in establishing the healthy relationship habits that will see your marriages through those difficult-to-navigate seasons of life.

The notion of consummation within a marriage has varied across cultures and traditions throughout history. It typically refers to the first sexual intercourse between a newly married couple, symbolizing the physical union and the completion of the marriage contract. However, it is important to note that the significance placed on consummation can differ depending on cultural, religious, and personal beliefs.

In some cultures, consummation is considered a crucial aspect of a marital relationship, as it is believed to solidify the bond between the couple and fulfill the expectations of a valid marriage. This perspective often stems from religious teachings or traditional values that prioritize the physical expression of love and the procreative aspect of marriage.

However, it is essential to recognize that the significance of consummation may vary among individuals and communities. Not all couples place the same emphasis on the act itself, as the spiritual and emotional connection between partners can be seen as equally important or even more significant.

Ultimately, the importance of consummation within a marriage is subjective and based on personal, cultural, and religious beliefs. Couples need to have open and honest communication about their expectations and values regarding this aspect of their relationship, respecting each other's perspectives and finding common ground that aligns with their mutual understanding of the physical and spiritual aspects of their union.

The Calming Tide Of Femininity And Sisterhood

The transition into expanding your family is so much smoother when your initial wife is happy, confident, and willing to move forward in the direction you are leading your family.

Initial wives will come to realize that cultivating a relationship with the incoming wife will go a lot smoother when kindness, empathy, and compassion are extended.

Creating a harmonious family dynamic and fostering positive relationships between wives in a polygynous arrangement is detrimental to the overall success of the family.

From the outset, all parties involved should engage in open and honest communication. This includes expressing feelings, concerns, and expectations. Clear and respectful communication can help in understanding each other's perspectives and finding common ground.

Generally, women are naturally gentle, calm, assertive, and understanding. When trust and open communication are threatened or removed from the equation, we begin to see an increased rise in toxicity and unhealthy behaviors.

Trust and open communication are indeed essential components of healthy relationships, regardless of gender. When these elements are lacking, it can lead to increased conflict, misunderstanding, and toxicity.

Building trust and maintaining open lines of communication requires effort and commitment from all parties involved. It is crucial to foster an environment where everyone feels safe to express themselves, listen to each other's perspectives, and work through challenges respectfully and constructively.

In any relationship, it is important to recognize and address toxic or unhealthy behaviors, regardless of their structure. Toxic behaviors can manifest in various ways, such as manipulation, disrespect, control, or emotional abuse. It is necessary to set boundaries, seek support if needed, and prioritize the well-being and safety of all individuals involved.

Each wife should be treated with respect and dignity. This involves acknowledging their individual needs, feelings, and contributions within the Divine Family Unit. Respecting boundaries and actively listening to each other's viewpoints fosters a sense of appreciation and understanding.

Your initial wife will more than likely feel extremely vulnerable during the beginning phases of your journey into polygyny. Even if she seems to be okay with your decision to expand your family, you mustn't disregard any signs of emotional unease.

The importance of reading between the lines and identifying the areas of communication that can be strengthened is something you will have to intentionally address as the leader of your family.

When your initial wife realizes that you are serious about your decision to expand the family, it will cause her to reflect, and question if she has lost value in your eyes. It is highly suggested that you reassure her and let her know that she holds great significance in your life.

Expanding your family means that you are adding and multiplying upon the foundation you've created and established with your initial wife. Many people make the mistake of assuming that expanding means subtracting and dividing a family.

Creating a well-balanced and peaceful environment in your relationship can indeed have a positive impact on spouses, way before polygyny is ever mentioned. When there is harmony and balance, it can inspire and motivate individuals to bring out their best selves and contribute to the relationship with love, attention, and a sense of calmness and serenity.

While it is important to recognize and appreciate the unique qualities and strengths that your wife brings to the relationship, it is crucial to remember that individual experiences and personalities are complex and shaped by a variety of factors beyond just gender. Each person's behavior and tendencies are influenced by their upbringing, personal experiences, cultural background, and individual temperament.

This means that you can read all of the material, and watch all of the self-help content about polygyny that you desire, but you must always keep in mind that other people's experiences won't be those of your own.

It is essential to foster an environment of mutual respect, open communication, and support where spouses can thrive and contribute to the relationship's well-being. Encouraging your initial wife's personal growth, validating her emotions, actively listening to her, and showing appreciation for her efforts can further strengthen the bond between you.

Remember that effective communication, understanding, and shared goals are key to building a fulfilling and balanced relationship. Emphasizing the qualities that contribute to a positive marriage, such as empathy, kindness, and emotional support, can create a nurturing environment where spouses can thrive and contribute to each other's happiness and well-being.

Being careful not to overly generalize, an environment that is well-balanced and peaceful will inspire and motivate your wife to be her best self. When she is at her best she will gladly and willingly apply love and attention to your relationship with a nourishing sense of calmness and serenity, which stems from her natural femininity.

Encouraging a sense of sisterhood between wives can be beneficial for the overall well-being of the family. Cultivating shared interests, engaging in activities together, and creating opportunities for bonding can help build stronger connections and a supportive environment.

Early on, you want to establish a communication protocol between your initial wife and your incoming wife. You could utilize texting, video chat, or phone calls. Do your best not to be frustrated when things seem to go differently than you expected. There may be misunderstandings that arise from different personality types, or statements made that get lost in translation. Your job is to make sure that you iron any misunderstandings out, and maintain the shalom of the family. Don't expect your family's year one, to be the same as another family's year ten.

Both women will greatly appreciate your efforts, even when it doesn't seem like it at first. Allowing them to communicate will reassure both of them that you aren't being slithery or conniving. You will be able to illustrate your vision to them, and they will be able to connect from a sisterly perspective which will increase the harmony within your family.

Recognizing and validating each other's emotions is essential for maintaining a healthy relationship. You will have to work overtime to showcase to both women that you understand this important element of relationship building. Showing empathy and compassion allows for a deeper understanding of each other's experiences and promotes a more nurturing and caring atmosphere.

Ensuring fairness and equality among wives is crucial in avoiding feelings of jealousy or resentment. It's important to establish equitable guidelines regarding time, resources, and decision-making processes within the family structure. Be flexible with your approach. Promote inclusion within your decision-making process, but make it clear that all final decisions will be made by you.

Lastly, seek professional guidance if needed. In complex family dynamics, seeking the assistance of a professional therapist or counselor who specializes in polygynous relationships can be beneficial. They can provide guidance, support, and mediation during challenging times. One of the world's leading resources for polygynous advice and counseling is Outstanding Personal Relationships, founded by Coach Nazir, and his wonderful co-wives, Coaches Fatimah and Nyla.

Remember, every relationship is unique, and what works for one family may not work for another. It's important to adapt these principles to your specific circumstances, values, and beliefs while maintaining a strong commitment to open communication, respect, and understanding.

-True Ju

Acknowledgement

To my beloved family,

This dedication is a testament to the profound journey we have embarked upon together, as we delve into the depths of the Divine Family. Inspired by the wisdom of Biblical polygyny, this book is dedicated to each of you who've embraced the idea of an expanded family strategy.

Your unwavering support and unwavering commitment have been the pillars upon which this exploration has flourished. Through the pages of this book, we have discovered a unique perspective, an insight that has shed light on the historical and Biblical significance of polygyny. Together, we have unraveled its complexities and delved into the practicalities of this age-old tradition.

In the pursuit of knowledge, we have grappled with challenges and found solace in our shared experiences. I've done my best to provide a balanced and thorough analysis, drawing upon Biblical examples and historical sources, which has fortified our understanding. We have learned to navigate the intricacies of jealousy, foster open and honest communication, and manage our household's financial well-being with grace.

Yet, it is the practicality of this journey that has truly transformed our lives. Within these pages lies a roadmap to building an expanded family strategy that works—a guide to finding and courting potential wives, nurturing financial stability, and to establishing the foundations of a healthy and harmonious family.

Whether we began as novices or seasoned leaders, this book has equipped us with invaluable insights and practical wisdom. Through its pages, we have embraced the multifaceted tapestry of polygyny, gaining a deeper appreciation for its complexities and the blessings it can bestow upon our lives.

To each member of our Divine Family Unit, I offer my deepest gratitude for embracing this exploration with an open heart. May this dedication serve as a reminder of our unwavering commitment to each other and the pursuit of knowledge, as we continue to grow and thrive together.

With boundless love and gratitude,

-Papa

1

RECOGNIZING POLYGYNY IN THE SCRIPTURES

What Is Polygyny?

Polygyny is a form of marriage in which a man has multiple wives. There are several claimed benefits of polygyny, some of which are:

1. **Economic benefits:** In societies where polygyny is practiced, men are expected to provide for their wives and children. Having multiple wives can increase the household's economic output, as more people are contributing to the household's income.

2. **Social benefits:** Polygyny can provide social benefits, such as increased social status for the man and his family. It can also create extended families, which can provide emotional support and help with child-rearing.

3. **Reproductive benefits:** Polygyny can lead to an increase in the number of children a man has, which can be advantageous in societies where having many children is seen as a sign of

wealth and success.

4. **Security benefits:** Polygyny can provide security for women who might otherwise be left without support. In societies where women are not allowed to own property or inherit from their families, having a husband who can provide for them can be crucial.

It is worth noting, however, that while these benefits may exist in some societies, polygyny is also associated with several potential drawbacks, including gender inequality, the exploitation of women, and the spread of sexually transmitted infections. Additionally, many societies have moved away from polygynous practices, as they are often seen as outdated and unfair to women.

Polygyny: A Cultural Norm Throughout Biblical History

The practice of biblical men having multiple wives is a topic of much debate and controversy. It is a topic that has been discussed for centuries, with various scholars and theologians offering different interpretations of the texts and their meanings. In this chapter, we will explore the story of biblical men having many wives, its historical and cultural context, and its relevance in modern times.

The practice of polygyny, or having multiple wives, is prevalent throughout the Tanakh, also known as the Old Testament or the Scriptures, and was common in the ancient region of Northeast Africa, as well as throughout the interior regions of Africa. Polygyny was also practiced by many of the Biblical patriarchs. The first recorded instance of polygamy in the Bible is found in Genesis 4:19, where Lamech takes two wives. From there, the practice of polygyny is mentioned several times in the Old Testament. Many of the Biblical patriarchs, such as Abraham, Jacob, and David, are depicted as having multiple wives.

The Bible does not explicitly condemn the practice of polygyny, and in fact, some passages condone it. For example, Deuteronomy 21:15-17 states that if a man has two wives, one whom he loves and one whom he dislikes, he must still give both wives equal rights, and follow a specific protocol in regards to the children they produce, as his heirs.

However, other passages in the Bible seem to suggest that polygyny was not God's ideal structure for marriage. In Genesis 2:24, it is stated that "a man shall leave his father and his mother and hold fast to his wife, and they shall become one flesh." This passage seems to imply that marriage should be between one man and one woman, not between one man and multiple women. Furthermore, in the New Testament, the Apostle Paul writes that church leaders should be "the husband of one wife" (1 Timothy 3:2), indicating that monogamy was the preferred marital arrangement for early leaders of the church.

What we will discuss in this work is the truth of the matter: that a man is permitted to have more than one wife, and that he is marrying each wife monogamously, with the overall family collective residing under the umbrella of what society refers to as polygyny. We will refer to this ancient family structure as The Divine Family Unit.

We will come to realize that when a man marries multiple women, those women are not marrying one another. It is the man that bridges the connection between all of the women who are members of The Divine Family Unit. Much of the confusion perpetrated by modern society regarding polygyny stems from an erroneous perspective on what polygyny is or isn't.

3

The practice of polygyny in the Old Testament can be understood within its historical and cultural context. In ancient times, having multiple wives was often seen as a sign of wealth and power. It was also a way to ensure the continuation of a man's family line, as each wife could bear him children. Additionally, in a culture where women had few rights and protections, having multiple wives may have been a way for men to provide for and protect more women.

However, the practice of polygyny also led to many problems and conflicts. In the story of Jacob and his two wives, Rachel and Leah, we see jealousy and competition between the two women. Similarly, in the story of David and his many wives, we see how his relationships with them often caused strife and division within his family.

In modern times, the practice of polygyny is illegal in most countries and is generally considered unethical and harmful. Many argue that polygyny is inherently unequal, as it places one man in a position of power over multiple women. Additionally, polygynous relationships often result in emotional and psychological harm to the women involved, as well as to any children they may have.

This book explores the topic of biblical men having multiple wives, also known as polygyny, and its historical and cultural context, as well as its relevance in modern times. While the Tanakh depicts many Biblical patriarchs, such as Abraham, Jacob, and David, as having multiple wives, the Bible, in truth, does not explicitly condemn the practice. The Bible endorses polygyny in many instances with God Himself taking part in this Divine Family structure.

We read in Jeremiah 31:31-33 NKJV "Behold, the days are coming, says YaHeWaHe, when I will make a new covenant with the house of Israel and with the house of Judah; {32} "not according to the covenant that I made with their fathers in the day that I took them by the hand to lead them out of

4

the land of Egypt, My covenant which they broke, though **I was a husband to them**, says YaHeWaHe. {33} "But this is the covenant that I will make with the house of Israel after those days, says YaHeWaHe: I will put My law in their minds, and write it on their hearts, and I will be their God, and they shall be My people."

However, some passages suggest that monogamy was God's ideal for marriage. The practice of polygyny was prevalent in ancient times and was often seen as a sign of wealth and power, as well as a way to ensure the continuation of a man's family line. In modern times, polygyny is generally considered unethical and harmful, as it often results in inequality and emotional and psychological harm to women and children. Ultimately, the focus should be on promoting healthy and equal relationships between partners, regardless of their gender or number.

The story of biblical men having many wives is a complex and controversial topic that has been the subject of much discussion and debate over the years. While some people view this practice as a traditional and acceptable part of the Biblical culture, others see it as a problematic and patriarchal aspect of ancient societies.

The Old Testament, in particular, contains numerous examples of men who had multiple wives. Perhaps the most well-known example is King Solomon, who is said to have had 700 wives and 300 concubines. According to 1 Kings 11:3, Solomon did have 700 wives and 300 concubines. While some have speculated that this number is an exaggeration or a symbolic representation of Solomon's wealth and power, it is clear that he had many wives and concubines.

Other notable figures who had multiple wives include Abraham, Jacob, and David, but they are not the only recorded examples that we can read about within the Scriptures.

The Bible often portrays the negative consequences of polygyny, such as the worship of strange gods, jealousy, rivalry, and division within families. For example, the story of Solomon, although filled with excellency and achievements, has a rather bitter ending, where he began to marry wives who were not of his tribe. These foreign wives began to influence Solomon away from serving the God of Israel.

His worship of strange and foreign gods, introduced to him by his foreign wives, marked the end of the unification of the Kingdom of Israel and proved to be disastrous for the people of Israel. Solomon's downfall began when he disobeyed the commandment to not marry women of other nations (Deuteronomy 7:3-4), and not because he was polygynous as some would like to suggest. Another example is the story of Jacob and his two wives, Leah and Rachel, which is one of competition and strife, with each wife vying for Jacob's attention and favor.

The Bible also guides how to properly conduct polygynous relationships. In Deuteronomy 21:15-17, it is stated that a man who has two wives must treat both wives equally and cannot show favoritism to one over the other. However, this guidance is often ignored or violated in the biblical accounts of polygynous relationships.

The cultural and historical context in which these relationships existed must also be taken into account. In the ancient region of Northeast Africa, polygyny was often a way for men to demonstrate their wealth and power, as well as to ensure that their lineage carried on into the future. Polygynous households also illustrated to the community of the time, that a man was a leader and had vision.

Many of the cultural connotations of polygyny were stripped from Israelite men upon their enslavement throughout the world. Now that Israelite men have awakened to their true identity, it is no wonder there has been an upsurge and desire to return to this Divine and ancestral custom, and way of life.

It is important to note that the Bible does not necessarily condemn the practice of having multiple wives. However, many of the stories that involve polygyny are accompanied by negative consequences and moral lessons. For example, in the story of Jacob and his first two wives, Rachel and Leah, the jealousy and rivalry between the two women is a major theme that ultimately leads to a great deal of conflict and pain.

King David, who is considered one of the most important figures in the Hebrew Bible, is said to have had many wives and concubines. The Bible records at least eight wives of David, including Bathsheba, whom he famously seduced and then arranged to have her husband Uriah killed. This story highlights the complex power dynamics between men and women in ancient Near Eastern culture, as well as the consequences of adultery and betrayal.

Furthermore, at least at first glance, the New Testament is largely silent on the issue of polygyny, except for a few passages that emphasize the importance of monogamous relationships. In the Gospel of Matthew, for instance, Yahewasha (whom the majority of the world ignorantly refers to as Jesus) quotes the Book of Genesis when he says, "Therefore a man shall leave his father and his mother and hold fast to his wife, and they shall become one flesh" (Matthew 19:5). Upon deeper analyzation, the reader will soon realize that even the New Testament is jam-packed with polygynous connotations. A huge theme and example of the New Testament polygynous undertones are derived from HaMasiach's (Christ's) marriage to the church.

Even though many people believe that polygyny is not explicitly endorsed in the Bible, the practice did play a significant role in ancient societies, particularly in Northeast Africa. A true studier of The Word would eventually have to ask the serious question: did polygyny even *need* to be endorsed, and is that why we don't see instructions from God saying

7

"Man, take unto yourself multiple women to make them wives to yourself"? A man's natural proclivity is to have many women, no different than it's a human's natural proclivity to drink water, and yet, there is nowhere commanded in the Scriptures to drink water eight times a day for instance because that is a healthy practice we commit to if we want our bodies to function properly. There are, however, Scriptural instructions for a man who would like to lead multiple women as his wives. In many cases, having multiple wives was seen as a sign of wealth and power, and it was often used as a means of forging political alliances and cementing relationships between different tribes and clans.

In modern times, the practice of polygyny is still found in many cultures, particularly in regions located within the interior, West, and East coasts of Africa, as well as Northeast Africa. However, it is generally viewed as a controversial and outdated practice in Western societies, where monogamy is the norm. It must be noted that Romanticism is the leading frame of mind, and is not the same as Hebraic thought, so one must consider this when indulging in the melting pot known as The West today.

These two extremely different thought forms must be considered when culture and identity are mentioned. When a people from a pre-existing culture are taken captive and removed from their ancestral customs, and then Divinely reintroduced to them, there will be a deep desire to take back what was stolen away from them. Polygyny practiced by Israelites in modern times, especially in the West, is a direct response to this.

Overall, the story of biblical men having many wives is a complex and multifaceted topic that continues to generate debate and discussion. While the Bible does contain numerous examples of polygamous relationships, it is important to view these stories in their historical and cultural context and to consider the moral lessons that they convey.

As we are beginning to realize, the story of Biblical men having many wives is a complex and controversial topic. While the Bible does not explicitly condemn the practice of polygyny, it also does not paint it as being the ready choice for every man regarding marriage. The practice can be openly understood within its historical and cultural context, but its relevance in modern times is purposely misunderstood.

Ultimately, the focus should be on promoting healthy and equitable relationships between spouses, regardless of the timing of their entry into the family or the number of members which comprise the expanded family dynamic.

2

ABRAHAM AND HIS THREE WIVES

T his chapter discusses the story of Abraham and his three wives - Sarah, Hagar, and Keturah - as told in the book of Genesis in the Bible. Abraham is considered the patriarch of Judaism, Christianity, and Islam and is known for his strong faith and obedience to God. Sarah was Abraham's first wife, and despite being barren for many years, she eventually gave birth to Isaac.

Hagar, an Egyptian servant given to Abraham by Sarah, gave birth to Ishmael, who became the father of the Arab people. Sarah's mistreatment of Hagar led to tension between the two women. Abraham married Keturah after Sarah's death, and she bore him six children.

Sarah, Hagar, and Keturah are the three wives of Abraham, the patriarch of many nations, and a significant figure in the Abrahamic religions.

The historical narrative illustrates the complexities, and the blessings, of polygynous relationships and Abraham's faith and obedience to God's will.

Abraham And His Three Wives

The story of Abraham and his three wives is a significant aspect of the Abrahamic religions, particularly in Judaism, Christianity, and Islam. Abraham is considered the patriarch of these religions and is known for his strong faith and obedience to God.

According to the biblical account in the book of Genesis, Abraham had three wives: Sarah, Hagar, and Keturah.

Sarah was Abraham's first wife and his half-sister (Genesis 11:29, 20:1-14). She was barren for many years, but God promised her that she would bear a son and that her descendants would be as numerous as the stars in the sky. Despite her advanced age, Sarah eventually gave birth to Isaac (Genesis 21:1-2), who became the father of Jacob, who was later renamed Israel.

Hagar was an Egyptian servant who belonged to Sarah (Genesis 16). When Sarah was unable to conceive a child, she gave Hagar to Abraham as a wife so that she could bear him a child. Hagar gave birth to Ishmael, who became the father of the Arab people.

However, Sarah became jealous of Hagar and mistreated her, which led to Hagar running away. God appeared to Hagar and promised her that her son would also become a great nation. Eventually, Hagar returned to Abraham and Sarah's household, but the tension between the two women remained.

Keturah was Abraham's third wife, whom he married after Sarah's death (Genesis 25:1-2). Keturah bore Abraham six children, and they were sent away to live in the East.

Abraham's story is a testament to his faith in God and his obedience to His will. Despite the challenges he faced, including his lack of an heir, he remained faithful and trusted in God's promise to make his descendants numerous. The story of Abraham and his three wives also illustrates the complexities and difficulties of polygynous relationships, which were common in ancient times but are not condoned in modern times.

Abraham, Father Of Many Nations

Abraham is one of the most important figures in the history of monotheistic religions, and his story is told in the Bible, the Quran, and the Torah. He is known as the "father of many nations" and is revered in Judaism, Christianity, and Islam.

According to the biblical account, Abraham was called by God to leave his homeland of Ur and travel to Canaan, where God promised him that he would become the father of a great nation. Abraham obeyed God's call and left with his wife Sarah, his nephew Lot, and his possessions.

As they journeyed, Abraham faced many trials and tribulations, including famine, war, and the loss of his wife's fertility. However, he remained faithful to God and trusted in His promise to make him the father of many nations.

After years of waiting, Sarah gave birth to a son, Isaac, who became the father of Jacob, who was later renamed Israel. God tested Abraham's faith by asking him to sacrifice Isaac, but at the last moment, God provided a ram for the sacrifice instead.

Abraham's story is seen as a model of faith and obedience to God, and his legacy has continued through the generations. In Islam, Abraham is known as Ibrahim and is considered one of the greatest prophets, alongside

Moses and Yahewasha. Muslims believe that Abraham was the first person to believe in the one God and that he rebuilt the Kaaba in Mecca, which remains a central site of pilgrimage in Islam.

Abraham's story also has important implications for modern-day issues, including the relationship between Jews, Christians, and Muslims and the conflict in the Middle East. Despite the divisions that exist between these groups, they all share a common heritage in the story of Abraham, and his legacy continues to inspire people of faith all over the world.

Sarah, The Beautiful Wife Of Abraham

Sarah, also known as Sarai, was the wife of Abraham and one of the matriarchs of Judaism, Christianity, and Islam. She is known for her beauty, her faith, and her loyalty to her husband.

According to the biblical account in the book of Genesis, Sarah was Abraham's half-sister and his first wife. She was known for her exceptional beauty, which caused Abraham to fear that he would be killed by the rulers of the lands they traveled through. To protect himself, he told them that Sarah was his sister, rather than his wife.

Sarah's beauty was not her only notable trait. She was also a woman of great faith, who believed in God's promise to make her husband the father of many nations. Despite being barren for many years, she continued to believe in God's promise and prayed for a child.

When Sarah was past childbearing age, God appeared to her and promised that she would bear a son. True to His promise, Sarah gave birth to Isaac, who became the father of Jacob, the patriarch of the twelve tribes of Israel.

Sarah's loyalty to her husband was also evident in her relationship with Hagar, Abraham's concubine. When Sarah was unable to conceive, she gave Hagar to Abraham as a wife so that she could bear him a child. However, after Hagar gave birth to Ishmael, Sarah became jealous and mistreated her. God appeared to Hagar and promised her that her son would also become a great nation.

Despite her imperfections, Sarah's faith and loyalty have made her an important figure in the history of Judaism, Christianity, and Islam. In Judaism, she is known as the mother of the Israelite people, and in Islam, she is considered a prophetess and a righteous woman.

Sarah's story also highlights the importance of faith, patience, and loyalty in the face of adversity. Despite the challenges she faced, she remained faithful to God and loyal to her husband, and her legacy has continued to inspire people of faith for thousands of years.

Hagar, And The Divine Gift Of Life

Hagar is a significant figure in the Abrahamic religions and the wife of Abraham who bore him a son named Ishmael. Her story is particularly important in Islam, where she is revered as a prophetess and a symbol of faith and endurance.

According to the biblical account in the book of Genesis, Hagar was an Egyptian servant who belonged to Sarah, Abraham's wife. When Sarah was unable to conceive a child, she gave Hagar to Abraham as a wife so that she could bear him a child. Hagar became pregnant with Ishmael, and Sarah became jealous and mistreated her.

Hagar eventually fled from Sarah's household and wandered in the wilderness, where she encountered an angel of YaHeWaHe who told her to return to Abraham and Sarah's household. The angel also promised that her son would become a great nation. Hagar returned and gave birth to Ishmael, who became the father of the Arab people.

In Islamic tradition, Hagar is considered a prophetess and a symbol of faith and endurance. Muslims believe that she demonstrated great faith in God and trusted in His plan for her life, even in the face of hardship and persecution. The story of Hagar and Ishmael is also an important part of the Hajj, the annual pilgrimage to Mecca that is one of the Five Pillars of Islam.

Hagar's story is a testament to the importance of faith and endurance in the face of adversity. Despite being a slave and being mistreated by her mistress, she remained faithful and trusted in God's plan for her life. Her legacy has continued to inspire people of faith for thousands of years, and her story is an important part of the Abrahamic traditions.

Keturah, The Blessed Mother Of Many

Keturah is a relatively lesser-known wife of Abraham, who is mentioned in the Hebrew Bible in the book of Genesis. She was married to Abraham after the death of his first wife Sarah and bore him six children.

According to the biblical account, after the death of Sarah, Abraham took another wife named Keturah, who was likely a concubine or a secondary wife. The book of Genesis mentions that Keturah bore Abraham six children, including Zimran, Jokshan, Medan, Midian, Ishbak, and Shuah.

The names of Keturah's children indicate that they became the ancestors of various tribes in the Middle East, particularly in Arabia. For example, Midian is believed to have been the ancestor of the Midianites, who are mentioned frequently in the Hebrew Bible.

The story of Keturah illustrates the importance of fertility and procreation in ancient societies, particularly in the context of family lineage and inheritance. Keturah's children were significant not only because they were Abraham's offspring, but also because they became the ancestors of various tribes and peoples in the Middle East.

While Keturah is not as well-known as Sarah or Hagar in the Abrahamic traditions, her story is an important reminder of the role of women in ancient societies and the significance of motherhood and procreation.

The lives of Sarah, Hagar, and Keturah illustrate the complexities and difficulties of polygynous relationships that were common in ancient times. The story of Sarah demonstrates the importance of faith and obedience to God's will. Hagar's story is particularly significant in Islam, where she is revered as a prophetess and a symbol of faith and endurance. Keturah's story illustrates the significance of fertility and procreation in ancient societies and the role of women in family lineage and inheritance.

Seeing Life Differently Than Others

Overall, the lives of these three wives of Abraham provide insight into the social, cultural, and religious practices of ancient societies and continue to inspire people of faith across the world.

Expanding our family isn't, and shouldn't be seen as a mistake. However, there are a series of methods, known as best practices in the corporate world, which we can implement to keep purposeful mistakes at a minimum. To see life differently, as Abraham did, and inspire people despite complex social, cultural, and religious practices in this modern-day paradigm, consider the following:

1. **Embrace diversity:** Recognize and appreciate the differences in culture, religion, and social practices. Be open-minded and willing to learn from others. By understanding and respecting different perspectives, you can broaden your horizons and inspire others to do the same.

2. **Focus on common ground:** Despite differences, there are often common values and goals that people share. Highlight these similarities and use them as a starting point for communication and collaboration. This can help bridge gaps and bring people together.

3. **Lead by example:** Inspire others by living your own life in a positive and meaningful way. Show kindness, compassion, and respect to everyone you encounter, regardless of their background or beliefs. Be authentic to yourself, and others will be drawn to your positive energy.

4. **Use storytelling:** Storytelling is a powerful way to inspire people and communicate complex ideas. Use personal experiences or examples from history and literature to illustrate your message and make it more relatable.

5. **Be creative:** Use creative approaches to inspire people and challenge the status quo. Art, music, and other forms of expression can help break down barriers and bring people together in a unique way.

6. **Practice empathy:** Try to understand the perspectives and emotions of others, including those in your family who may have different beliefs or practices. Empathy can help build bridges and create deeper connections, even in the face of differences.

7. **Communicate openly and honestly:** Be willing to have difficult conversations with your family members, but do so with respect and

kindness. Honest communication can help break down misunderstandings and create a more harmonious environment.

8. **Focus on shared values:** Despite differences, there may be shared values or goals that you and your family members hold dear. Identify these commonalities and focus on them as a way to connect and inspire each other.

9. **Lead by example:** Be a role model for your family members by living according to your values and principles. Be kind, compassionate, and respectful, even in the face of challenges or adversity. Your positive example can inspire others to do the same.

10. **Find common ground:** Seek out areas where you and your family members can agree and work together towards a common goal. This can help create a sense of unity and purpose, even in the face of complex social, cultural, and religious practices.

A loving father will always want the next generation descending from him, to be better than he is. As righteous as Abraham was, we have the opportunity as his descendants, to be just as righteous, if not greater. As long as we learn from the mistakes he made, while simultaneously applying the methods that he got correct, we will be on a path to guiding our family properly.

By incorporating these strategies into your interactions with your family members and personal daily experience, you can see life differently and inspire others despite the complex social, cultural, and religious practices in our modern world. Remember, when Abraham and his wives were living, there were complexities surrounding the social norms of their day.

We tend to look at occurrences in the past as long-forgotten moments in history that don't have any active effect on how we operate today. If we learn from the mistakes made in the past, we can apply the lessons that those mistakes inspired, to our lives today.

We also need to remember to approach these interactions with an open mind and heart and to always seek to understand and empathize with all of the members of our Divine Family Unit.

3

THE STORY OF JACOB AND HIS FOUR WIVES

The story of Jacob and his four wives is a fascinating tale of love, deception, and redemption that is told in the book of Genesis in the Bible. Jacob was the son of Isaac and Rebekah and the grandson of Abraham, who was one of the great patriarchs of the Hebrew People, including the Israelites. Jacob had twelve sons, who became the twelve tribes of Israel, and a daughter named Dinah.

The story begins with Jacob falling in love with Rachel, the younger daughter of Laban, his mother's brother. Jacob agreed to work for Laban for seven years in exchange for Rachel's hand in marriage. However, on the wedding night, Laban deceived Jacob by giving him Leah, Rachel's older sister, instead. Jacob was furious but agreed to work another seven years for Rachel, whom he loved deeply.

Jacob's love for Rachel did not diminish, but she was barren while Leah had given him several sons. Rachel, desperate for children, gave her handmaid, Bilhah, to Jacob as a wife, and she bore him two sons, Dan and Naphtali. Leah, who was also barren after birthing four sons, Reuben, Simon, Levi, and Judah, for Jacob, gave her handmaid, Zilpah, to Jacob, and she bore him two more sons, Gad and Asher.

Leah, although unloved by Jacob at times, gave birth to Jacob's eldest sons, one of which was Levi, who would come to be known as the Priestly tribe from whom Moses, Aaron, and Miriam would descend, as well as Judah, who would come to be known as the tribe from which YaHeWaShA HaMashiach would descend.

Rachel eventually gave birth to two sons, Joseph and Benjamin, but tragically died during childbirth. Jacob was heartbroken and buried Rachel in the land of Canaan. However, he still had four wives and many children to care for.

The relationships between the wives and their children were complex and often fraught with jealousy and competition. The children of Leah and Rachel often vied for their father's attention and affection. Joseph, the favorite son of both Rachel and Jacob, was despised by his brothers, who sold him into slavery in Egypt. However, Joseph eventually rose to power in Egypt and was able to rescue his family from a devastating famine.

Despite the challenges and difficulties, the story of Jacob and his four wives shows that God's plan for redemption and restoration can still be fulfilled even amid deception and betrayal. Jacob's descendants, the Israelites, became a great nation, and through them, God's promise to bless all nations was fulfilled through the coming of YaHeWaShA HaMashiach.

Jacob And His Service For His Uncle Laban

Jacob's service for his uncle Laban is a significant part of the story of Jacob in the Bible. After fleeing from his brother Esau, who was angry with him for stealing his birthright and blessing, Jacob traveled to the land of Haran, where his mother's brother, Laban, lived.

Upon his arrival, Jacob met Rachel, Laban's younger daughter, and fell deeply in love with her. He agreed to work for Laban for seven years in exchange for Rachel's hand in marriage. However, on the wedding night, Laban deceived Jacob by giving him Leah, Rachel's older sister, instead.

Jacob was understandably angry and demanded that Laban give him Rachel as well. Laban agreed, but only if Jacob would work another seven years for him. Jacob agreed, and he worked hard for Laban during those years.

During his time working for Laban, Jacob became a successful shepherd, and God blessed him with many flocks and herds. However, Laban was a shrewd businessman and tried to cheat Jacob out of his fair share of the profits. He changed Jacob's wages ten times, but each time God intervened, and Jacob prospered.

Jacob also became the father of many children during his time working for Laban. Leah, who was initially given to Jacob by Laban, bore him six sons and a daughter. Rachel, who was Jacob's true love, was initially barren, but she eventually gave birth to two sons, Joseph and Benjamin.

Despite Laban's attempts to deceive and cheat him, Jacob remained faithful to his commitment to work for Laban. He honored his uncle, even when Laban was not honorable in his dealings with him. Eventually, after many years, Jacob decided to leave Laban and return to his homeland with his family and flock.

Jacob's service to his Uncle Laban was a time of great growth and learning for him. He became a successful shepherd, a loving husband, and a father of many children. Despite the challenges he faced, Jacob remained faithful and learned important lessons about perseverance, trust in God, and honoring one's commitments.

Jacob's name was changed to Israel by God after he wrestled with an angel in Genesis 32:28. The name "Israel" means "he who struggles with God" or "God strives". This event marked a turning point in Jacob's life, where he was transformed from a deceitful man into one who wrestled with God and prevailed. From this point on, he was known as Israel, and his descendants came to be known as the Israelites.

Rachel, The One Whom Jacob Loved

Rachel was one of the most important figures in the life of Jacob, the patriarch of the Israelite people. She was the younger daughter of Laban, Jacob's uncle, and the one whom Jacob loved deeply. The story of Rachel and Jacob is a tale of enduring love, hope, and tragedy.

Jacob fell in love with Rachel at first sight and agreed to work for her father, Laban, for seven years in exchange for her hand in marriage. However, on the wedding night, Laban tricked Jacob by giving him Leah, Rachel's older sister, instead. Jacob was angry but agreed to work for another seven years to earn Rachel's hand in marriage.

Rachel and Jacob's love for each other was deep and passionate. Rachel was described as being beautiful and graceful, and her presence lit up Jacob's life. Despite the challenges they faced, including Leah's jealousy and rivalry, Rachel and Jacob remained devoted to each other.

Rachel, however, was barren for many years, and this caused her great sadness and despair. She begged Jacob to give her children, but it was only after many years that she finally gave birth to Joseph, the first of her two sons. Rachel's joy at the birth of her son was immense, and she named him Joseph, meaning "God has added."

Tragically, Rachel died giving birth to her second son, Benjamin. She was buried on the side of the road in Bethlehem, and Jacob mourned her deeply. Her death was a great loss to Jacob, and he never forgot her. When he blessed his children before he died, he mentioned Rachel, saying, "I have loved Rachel more than Leah."

Rachel's story is a reminder that true love is enduring and steadfast, even in the face of hardship and tragedy. Her life also teaches us the importance of hope and faith in God, even amid great pain and sorrow.

Rachel was a beloved wife and mother who played an important role in the story of Jacob and the Israelite people. Her love for Jacob and her children was profound, and her life is a testimony to the power of love and hope in the face of adversity.

Leah, The Mother Of Praise

Leah was the older daughter of Laban and the first wife of Jacob, the patriarch of the Israelite people. Although she was initially overshadowed by her younger sister Rachel, Leah's story is one of resilience, faith, and ultimately, praise.

Leah was not the first choice for Jacob regarding marriage, and this made her feel unwanted and unloved. However, when Jacob arrived in Haran, Laban tricked him into marrying Leah instead of Rachel. Leah must have been aware of Jacob's love for Rachel, but she agreed to marry him anyway, hoping that he would eventually love her too.

Leah bore Jacob's six sons: Reuben, Simeon, Levi, Judah, Issachar, and Zebulun. She also bore him a daughter, Dinah. Although she was not the object of Jacob's love, Leah loved him deeply and remained faithful to him throughout her life.

Leah's story is one of resilience and faith. Despite feeling unloved and unwanted, she never lost hope or faith in God. She recognized that her worth was not based on Jacobs's desirability of her but on her inner character and her relationship with God.

Leah's faith in God was also evident in the names she gave her children. Each Hebraic name had a special meaning that reflected her trust in God and her gratitude for His blessings. For example, Reuben means "see, a son," and Simeon means "heard by God." Levi means "attached," and Judah means "now I praise YaHeWaHe."

Leah's life was not easy, but she remained faithful to God and Jacob. She supported him in his struggles and helped build the Israelite people's foundation. Her story teaches us about the importance of resilience, faith, and the recognition that our worth is not based on our popularity with others, but on our inner character and our relationship with God.

Leah was a strong and faithful woman who played an important role in the story of Jacob and the Israelite people. She was truly the mother of praise, for she praised God in all circumstances and gave thanks for His blessings.

Bilhah, The Wife Of Rachel's Redemption

Bilhah was a servant and handmaid of Rachel, the beloved second wife of Jacob, the patriarch of the Israelite people.

She played a significant role in the story of Jacob, as she became his third wife and bore him two sons, Dan and Naphtali. Bilhah's story is one of redemption and hope. She was a servant, owned by Laban, Rachel's father, and had no control over her own life or destiny. However, when Rachel was unable to have children, she gave Bilhah to Jacob as a wife, hoping that she would bear children in her place.

Bilhah's status as a wife was a significant redemption for her. It was a step up from being a servant and gave her more freedom and autonomy. Although she was not a beloved wife like Rachel, she was still valued by Jacob and bore him two sons.

Bilhah's story also teaches us about the importance of hope and perseverance. Despite her low status as a servant, Bilhah did not give up hope for a better life. She continued to serve Rachel faithfully, even when it was difficult, and ultimately, her faithfulness was rewarded with a higher status as a wife and the birth of two sons.

Bilhah's life reminds us that no matter how lowly our position may be, we should never give up hope for a better future. She is an example of a woman who persevered in difficult circumstances and was ultimately redeemed.

Although not much is known about Bilhah's personality or character, her story is a testament to her faithfulness and perseverance. She was a loyal and dedicated servant to Rachel, and her service ultimately led to her redemption. Her story reminds us that even the most difficult and challenging circumstances can lead to blessings and a better future.

Bilhah was a servant who became the third wife of Jacob and bore him two sons. Her story is a reminder of the importance of hope and perseverance and the potential for redemption, even in the most challenging circumstances. She is an example of a woman who remained faithful and dedicated, even in difficult circumstances, and ultimately, her faithfulness was rewarded with a higher status and the birth of two sons.

Zilpah, Elevated In Status

Zilpah was a handmaid of Leah, and the fourth wife of Jacob, the patriarch of the Israelite people. She played a significant role in the story of Jacob, as she became one of his wives and bore him two sons.

Zilpah was given to Leah as a handmaid by her father Laban. Leah gave her to Jacob as a wife, and she bore him two sons, Gad and Asher. Zilpah's status as a wife was elevated, and she was given a place of honor among Jacob's wives.

Zilpah's story is a reminder that in the ancient world, women were often viewed as property and were not always given the respect and honor they deserved. However, Zilpah's status as a wife shows that she was valued and honored by Jacob, even though she began her role in the family as a handmaid.

Zilpah's life also teaches us about the importance of serving others. She was a faithful and loyal handmaid to Leah, and her service ultimately led to her elevation in status. Her story is a reminder that even the most humble and lowly tasks can lead to great rewards and blessings.

Although not much is known about Zilpah's personality or character, her story is a testament to her faithfulness and loyalty to Leah and her willingness to serve others. Her life reminds us that sometimes the most important thing we can do is to serve others and to do so with humility and dedication.

Zilpah was a handmaid who became one of the four wives of Jacob and bore him two sons. Her story is a reminder of the importance of serving others and of the rewards that can come from faithful and dedicated service. She is an example of a woman who started from humble beginnings but was elevated in status due to her dedication and loyalty.

Strong Leadership

Jacob was a strong leader and patriarch of his family. Despite the complex relationships and rivalries between his wives and children, Jacob loved them all and worked hard to provide for and protect them. He was also known for his courage and perseverance, as evidenced by his many trials and struggles throughout his life, such as his conflict with his brother Esau and his journey to Laban's household. Ultimately, Jacob's leadership and faith in God played a crucial role in the formation of the twelve tribes of Israel and the fulfillment of God's promises to his descendants.

The reality of the situation between Jacob, his wives, and their many children, is certainly a challenging one, as managing complex family relationships can be a difficult task for any leader. However, here are some strategies you can use to be a strong leader despite the complexities of your family dynamics:

1. **Set clear expectations:** As the leader, it is your responsibility to establish clear expectations and boundaries for your family members. Be sure to communicate your expectations in a firm but compassionate manner, and hold all family members accountable for their actions

2. **Be fair and impartial:** It's important to treat all of your wives and children fairly and impartially, regardless of any rivalries or conflicts

that may exist. Avoid taking sides or showing favoritism, and make decisions based on what is best for the family as a whole.

3. **Encourage open communication:** Encourage all family members to express their thoughts and feelings openly and honestly, and make an effort to actively listen to everyone's perspectives. This can help to foster a more collaborative and supportive family dynamic.

4. **Practice conflict resolution:** Conflict is inevitable in any family, but as the leader, it's your responsibility to help resolve conflicts constructively and peacefully. Consider using techniques such as mediation, compromise, and active listening to help family members work through their differences.

5. **Lead by example:** Finally, the most effective way to be a strong leader is to lead by example. Model the behavior and attitudes you want to see in your family and demonstrate your commitment to creating a positive and supportive family environment.

6. **Respect individual differences:** Each wife and child in your family has their unique personality, needs, and strengths. Recognize and respect these differences, and make an effort to understand each family member on an individual level.

7. **Foster unity:** Despite the rivalries and conflicts that may exist within your family, strive to create a sense of unity and common purpose. Encourage family members to work together towards shared goals and to support each other through difficult times.

8. **Emphasize communication:** Communication is key to any successful family dynamic. Make an effort to encourage open and honest communication between all family members, and be willing to listen to everyone's perspectives and concerns.

9. **Seek guidance when needed:** It's okay to admit that you don't have all the answers. If you're struggling to manage the complexities of your family relationships, consider seeking guidance from a trusted advisor, such as a religious leader, therapist, or family counselor.

10. **Practice forgiveness:** Forgiveness is essential in any family dynamic. Encourage family members to practice forgiveness towards each other,

and model this behavior yourself. When conflicts arise, focus on finding a solution rather than assigning blame.

11. **Lead with love:** Ultimately, the most important thing you can do as a leader is to lead with love. Show your family members that you care about them deeply, and make an effort to demonstrate this love through your actions and words. By creating a positive and loving family environment, you can help your family overcome even the most complex challenges.

As men, we have to realize the reality of our decisions and stand on the choices we make. Our decision to expand our family is not a light one. Every member of the family is a living, breathing, vibrant Soul that must be guided and cultivated lovingly.

Assertiveness is important, but so is tenderness. The drive and desire to fulfill the vision placed onto our hearts by The Highest are important as well, but so is compassion. Practice and implement these techniques daily so that you can lead your Divine Family Unit into the absolute best possible life together.

4

THE STORY OF DAVID AND HIS MANY WIVES

David and The Kingdom Of Israel

The story of David is a complex one, filled with triumphs and tragedies. David was a man of great faith, a skilled warrior, and a gifted leader. He rose from humble beginnings as a shepherd boy to become the king of Israel, and he ruled with wisdom and compassion. However, David was also a flawed human being, and his story is filled with tales of betrayal, violence, and heartbreak.

One of the most fascinating aspects of David's story is his relationship with his wives. David had several wives throughout his life, and his relationships with them were complicated and sometimes fraught with conflict. Perhaps the most famous of David's wives was Bathsheba, whom he famously seduced and then arranged to have her husband killed. This scandalous affair brought great shame to David and his family, and it haunted him for the rest of his life.

However, Bathsheba was not the only wife in David's life. He had several other wives, including Michal, Abigail, and Ahinoam. Each of these women played a significant role in David's life, and their stories offer insight into the complexities of David's personal life.

Despite the challenges posed by his many wives, David was a successful ruler. He united the tribes of Israel and established Jerusalem as its capital. He was a wise and just king, and he was beloved by his people. He was also a man of great faith, and he wrote many of the Psalms that are still beloved by people all across the earth today.

Throughout his life, David faced many challenges and overcame many obstacles. He was an imperfect man, but he was also a man of great courage and conviction. He ruled Israel with compassion and guided his family with wisdom, and his legacy continues to inspire people today.

David and His Wives

David's first wife was Michal, the daughter of King Saul. David fell in love with Michal after he defeated Goliath and asked for her hand in marriage, but Saul was suspicious of David's intentions and demanded that he bring him the foreskins of one hundred Philistines as a dowry. David completed this task and was able to marry Michal, but their relationship was not always easy. Saul became jealous of David's success and turned against him, forcing David to flee for his life. During this time, Saul gave Michal to another man, and it was not until much later that David was reunited with her.

Saul was extremely jealous of David's success and attempted to kill him on several occasions, and Michal was caught in the middle of this conflict. Eventually, David was forced to flee from Saul and leave Michal behind.

David's second wife was Abigail, whom he married after her first husband, Nabal, died. While he was in hiding, David met Abigail, a beautiful and intelligent woman who was married to a wealthy man named Nabal. When Nabal refused to help David and his men, David planned to attack Nabal's household. However, Abigail intervened and convinced David to spare them. Impressed by her wisdom and bravery, David asked Abigail to become his wife. Abigail was a devoted wife to David and helped him in many ways throughout his life. Abigail was known for her intelligence and beauty, and she became one of David's most trusted advisors.

David also married Ahinoam, the daughter of a wealthy Israelite business-man, and several other women whose names are not mentioned in the Bible. However, it was David's relationship with Bathsheba that would become the most notorious, and have the most lasting impact on his life.

Bathsheba was the wife of Uriah, one of David's most loyal soldiers. Despite this, David seduced Bathsheba and arranged for Uriah to be called to the frontlines of a battle that the nation of Israel was engaged in. One day, while Bathsheba was bathing on a rooftop, David saw her and was overcome with desire. He arranged for Uriah to be sent to the front lines of battle, where he was killed, and then he took Bathsheba as his wife.

God was displeased with David's actions and sent the prophet Nathan to confront him. Nathan told David a story about a rich man who stole a poor man's only lamb, and David was incensed at the injustice. Nathan then revealed that the story was a metaphor for David's actions, and he prophesied that David's household would suffer as a result of his sin.

David was devastated by Nathan's words, and he spent the rest of his life trying to make amends for his actions. He remained a faithful servant of God and continued to rule Israel with wisdom and compassion. He also remained devoted to his family, even as they suffered the consequences of his sin.

David's story is a reminder of the power of faith and the consequences of sin. It is a complex tale of love, betrayal, and redemption, and it continues to inspire people today. Despite his flaws, David was a great leader and a man of great courage and conviction, and his legacy will endure for generations to come.

Michal, The Wife of Victory

Michal was the daughter of King Saul and the first wife of King David. According to the Bible, David fell in love with Michal after he killed Goliath, and King Saul promised to give him Michal in marriage if he could bring him 100 Philistine foreskins. David succeeded in this task and married Michal.

Michal played a significant role in David's life, especially during the early years of his reign. She was loyal to David and helped him to escape from her father, who had turned against him and was trying to kill him. Michal deceived her father by placing an image in David's bed to make it appear as if he was still there while David escaped through a window. She risked her safety and reputation to deceive her father and protect David, and her actions were instrumental in helping him to establish his kingdom.

However, Michal's relationship with David was not without its challenges. After David became king, he took several other wives, and Michal was given to another man. When David later became king again, he demanded that Michal be returned to him, but she had already been remarried and refused to leave her new husband. This was a significant event in Michal's story because it highlighted the way that women were often treated as property in ancient times. Michal was caught in a power struggle between two men who saw her as a commodity to be traded rather than a woman with personal desires and agency.

Michal's story is a complex one, and she is often portrayed as a tragic figure who was caught in the middle of the politics and power struggles between her father, King Saul, and her husband, King David. She was also mistreated by her second husband, who was chosen for her by her father after David fled from Saul's wrath. However, she remained loyal to David throughout her life, and her actions helped him to survive and thrive as king.

She played an important role in David's life, and her story is a reminder of the challenges faced by women in ancient times and the strength and resilience they demonstrated in the face of adversity. Michal continued to support David throughout his reign.

Abigail, The Wise, and Beautiful Wife

Abigail was a woman who played an important role in David's life. According to the Bible, Abigail was the wife of a wealthy man named Nabal who lived in the town of Carmel. When David and his men were on the run from King Saul, they stopped near Nabal's property and asked him for provisions. However, Nabal refused to help them, and David was so enraged that he planned to kill Nabal and all of his men.

Abigail, however, intervened and persuaded David to spare Nabal's life. She brought him and his men food and supplies, and she convinced David to forgive her husband's offense. When Nabal later died, David took Abigail as his wife.

Abigail was a woman of great intelligence and wisdom, and she was praised for her beauty and her ability to reason with David. She is often seen as a model of a virtuous and wise woman in the Bible, and her story highlights the importance of diplomacy and negotiation in resolving conflicts.

Abigail's role in David's life was significant. She became one of his wives and bore him a son named Chileab (also known as Daniel), who was the only son of David mentioned in the Bible who did not rebel against him. Abigail's intervention also helped to prevent a senseless act of violence and helped to cement David's reputation as a just and wise leader.

In addition, Abigail's story is a reminder of the important role that women played in ancient Israel, even in a largely patriarchal society. Abigail used her intelligence and her diplomatic skills to help save her husband's life and to prevent a tragedy, and her actions were instrumental in shaping David's life and legacy.

Ahinoam, The Wife Accustomed To Wealth

Ahinoam was the daughter of a wealthy Israelite businessman named Ahimaaz, and she became David's third wife. According to the Bible, David married Ahinoam while he was living in Ziklag, a town in the southern region of Judah.

Ahinoam's role in David's life is not as well-documented as that of some of his other wives, such as Bathsheba and Abigail. However, she was an important figure in David's life as a wife and mother to some of his children. She bore David two sons, Amnon and Kileab (also known as Daniel), who were both prominent figures in David's court.

Ahinoam's story highlights the importance of marriage and family in ancient Israel. Marriage was seen as a sacred institution, and a man's wives and children were considered to be an important part of his legacy. Ahinoam was a loyal and devoted wife to David, and she played an important role in helping to establish his dynasty.

Overall, while Ahinoam's story is not as well-known as some of David's other wives, she was an important figure in his life and played a significant role in helping him to build his legacy as a great king of Israel.

Bathsheba, More Than Beautiful; The Wife Of David's Desire

Bathsheba was the wife of Uriah the Hittite, a soldier in King David's army. She is best known for the scandalous affair she had with David, which ultimately led to Uriah's death and David's eventual repentance.

According to the Bible, David saw Bathsheba bathing on a rooftop and was overcome with desire for her. He summoned her to his palace, where they had an affair, even though Bathsheba was married to Uriah. When Bathsheba became pregnant, David tried to cover up his sin by summoning Uriah from the battlefield in the hopes that he would sleep with his wife and think that the child was his own. When Uriah refused to do so, David had him killed in battle.

After Uriah's death, David took Bathsheba as his wife. However, their first child died, and David was punished by God for his sins. Despite the scandal surrounding their relationship, Bathsheba remained loyal to David and bore him several more children, including Solomon, who would go on to become one of Israel's greatest kings.

Bathsheba's role in David's life is complex. While she was a victim of David's lust and betrayal, she also played a significant role in helping to establish David's dynasty. Her son Solomon succeeded David as king, and he went on to rule Israel with wisdom and justice.

Bathsheba's story is a reminder of the consequences of sin and the importance of repentance and forgiveness. While her relationship with David was scandalous and tragic, it ultimately led to the birth of Solomon and the establishment of his dynasty, which would play a major role in the history of Israel.

How To Handle Adversity Brought On By Our Own Decisions

David's story is a reminder that even the greatest leaders can be flawed and that it is possible to overcome our weaknesses and achieve greatness. Despite his sins and shortcomings, David is remembered as one of Israel's greatest kings, and his legacy continues to inspire people today. He was a man of great faith, a skilled warrior, and a gifted leader.

His wives often found themselves placed in the middle of his endeavors and didn't always get the fairest treatment.

Equity and equality amongst your wives are extremely important. Sometimes as men, we can let our desires and lustful ways get the better of us. When we make a lust-filled decision, it can be difficult to follow through on the responsibilities which that decision will create in our live's once the reality of that decision takes hold.

Life is full of decisions, and sometimes we make choices that lead to adversity. Whether it's a job we take, a relationship we enter into, or a path we choose to pursue, our decisions have consequences, both good and bad. It's easy to feel overwhelmed and defeated when we face the consequences of our choices, but it's important to remember that adversity is a part of life and that we can learn from it and grow stronger.

Here are some tips on how to handle adversity brought on by our own decisions:

1. **Take responsibility for your actions:** The first step in handling adversity brought on by your own decisions is to take responsibility for your actions. Acknowledge that you made a mistake and that you are responsible for the consequences. Blaming others or making excuses will only make the situation worse.

2. **Learn from your mistakes:** Adversity can be a great teacher, and the best way to learn from it is to reflect on your decisions and identify what went wrong. What factors influenced your decision-making? What could you have done differently? Use this information to make better decisions in the future.

3. **Don't beat yourself up:** It's easy to fall into a negative cycle of self-blame and self-pity, but this will only make things worse. Be kind to yourself and focus on moving forward. Remember that mistakes are a natural part of the learning process and that everyone makes them.

4. **Seek support:** Adversity can be isolating, but it's important to remember that you are not alone. Seek support from friends, family, or a therapist. Talking about your feelings and experiences can help you process them and move forward.

5. **Take action:** Once you've reflected on your decisions and learned from your mistakes, it's time to take action. What steps can you take to improve your situation? What changes can you make to ensure that you don't repeat the same mistakes? Taking action can help you feel empowered and in control of your life.

6. **Practice resilience:** Resilience is the ability to bounce back from adversity and come out stronger on the other side. Practice resilience

by cultivating a positive mindset, staying focused on your goals, and taking care of yourself both physically and mentally.

Handling adversity brought on by our own decisions can be challenging, but it's also an opportunity for growth and learning. Take responsibility for your actions, learn from your mistakes, seek support, take action, and practice resilience. Remember that adversity is a natural part of life and that you have the strength and resilience to overcome it.

In the case of an expanded family, adversity will arise, but each member of the Divine Family Unit is counting on you as the leader to figure out the best ways to deal with that adversity and move the family forward in a positive light.

5

THE STORY OF SOLOMON AND HIS MANY WIVES AND CONCUBINES

S olomon, the son of King David, is considered one of the most powerful and wealthy kings in the history of Israel. He is known for his wisdom, wealth, and his many wives and concubines. In this chapter, we will explore the story of Solomon and his many wives and concubines, and how he ruled the Kingdom of Israel while maintaining and guiding his family.

Solomon's Early Life

Solomon was born to King David and Bathsheba in Jerusalem, around 970 BC. He was the second son of David and Bathsheba, and was named Jedidiah, which means "beloved of the Lord." As a child, Solomon was known for his wisdom and was favored by God. When David was old and near death, he declared Solomon as his heir and commanded his officials to support him in his reign.

Solomon's Reign and His Many Wives and Concubines

Solomon's reign began when he was just 20 years old, and it lasted for 40 years. During his reign, he built the Temple in Jerusalem, which was considered a great achievement. He also strengthened the economy and expanded Israel's borders.

However, one of the most controversial aspects of Solomon's reign was his many wives and concubines. According to the Bible, Solomon had 700 wives and 300 concubines, who were from many different nations. This was in direct violation of God's commandment in Deuteronomy 7:3-4.

For those who would like to reference Deuteronomy 17:17, which states that "a king should not increase wives to himself, so as not to be led astray", keep in mind that that statute is referring to the king being provided for by The Highest who will Himself increase wives unto the king of Israel, as further referenced in 2 Samuel 12:8, "I gave your master's house to you, and your master's wives into your arms. I gave you all Israel and Judah. And if all this had been too little, I would have given you even more." This statement was made by The Most High through the prophet Nathan after David brought evil to the Kingdom of Israel by having Uriah killed so that he could marry Bathsheba. David was punished for his actions and Bathsheba would later give birth to Solomon.

Solomon's many wives and concubines caused him many problems, both personal and political. Some of his wives worshipped foreign gods, which led to Solomon worshipping them as well (Deuteronomy 7:3-4). This angered God, who warned Solomon that his actions would lead to the downfall of his kingdom.

Solomon's Legacy and Family

Solomon, also known as King Solomon, was a Biblical figure who ruled over Israel during the 10th century BCE. He is known for his wisdom and wealth, and his legacy has had a profound impact on Israelite, Christian, and Islamic traditions.

One of Solomon's most significant accomplishments was the construction of the Temple in Jerusalem. According to the Bible, God appeared to Solomon in a dream and offered him anything he wanted. Solomon chose wisdom, and God was pleased with his request, granting him not only wisdom but also wealth and power. With his newfound wisdom, Solomon was able to rule Israel with justice and equity, and his fame spread throughout the world.

Solomon's wealth and prosperity were legendary. He was known for his vast harem of wives and concubines, as well as his gold and silver mines and trade routes that spanned the ancient world. His wisdom and wealth attracted visitors and emissaries from all over the world, including the famous Queen of Sheba, who came to visit Solomon and test his wisdom.

Despite his many flaws, Solomon is remembered as one of the greatest kings in the history of Israel. He was known for his wisdom, wealth, and his many achievements. He also left behind a large family, which would go on to play an important role in the history of Israel.

Solomon's son, Rehoboam, succeeded him as king, but he faced a rebellion and lost control of many of the northern tribes of Israel to Jeroboam, one of Solomon's former officials, who was an Israelite from the tribe of Ephraim. This led to the split of the kingdom, with the northern tribes forming the Kingdom of Israel and the southern tribes forming the Kingdom of Judah.

The story of Solomon and his many wives and concubines is a complex one, just like the stories about the other patriarchs referenced in the Scriptures. While he is remembered as one of the greatest kings in the history of Israel, his actions also led to his downfall. Despite this, his legacy and family played an important role in the history of Israel, and he remains a revered figure in Hebraic Israelite and Christian tradition.

Solomon and His Wives

The story of Solomon and his wives is a fascinating one, filled with drama, intrigue, and controversy. Solomon, the son of David and Bathsheba, was known for his great wisdom and was the most powerful and wealthy king in the history of Israel, but one of the most controversial aspects of his reign was his many wives and concubines, which caused him both personal and political problems.

We will explore the story of Solomon and his wives, including their background, how he acquired them, and the impact they had on his reign.

Solomon's Wives

According to the Bible, Solomon had 700 wives and 300 concubines. These women came from many different nations, including Egypt, Moab, Ammon, Edom, and Sidon. Solomon's wives were chosen for many important reasons, as well as for personal desires. These reasons would culminate in the formation of political and strategic alliances with neighboring countries, and to satisfy Solomon's desires.

Solomon's wives were not all Israelites, and some of them worshipped foreign gods, which was a direct violation of God's commandments. These women influenced Solomon's beliefs and actions, leading him away from his faith in the one true God of Israel.

In the ancient world, marriage was often used as a way to form alliances between different nations. Kings and rulers would often marry the daughters of other kings to form a bond between their two countries. This was no different for Solomon, who married the daughters of many foreign kings to form alliances with their countries. However, it is clear that Solomon also had a strong desire for women. He was known for his wealth and power, and he used this to acquire many wives and concubines.

One of Solomon's most well-known wives was the daughter of Pharaoh, whom he married to seal a political alliance with Egypt. She was likely one of his first wives, and her presence in the royal court would have added to Solomon's prestige and power.

Another important wife of Solomon was the daughter of the king of Tyre. She was likely married to Solomon as part of a political alliance with the city of Tyre, which was an important center of trade and commerce in the ancient world.

Solomon's most famous wife was quite possibly the Queen of Sheba, who came to visit him and test his wisdom. She was impressed with his wisdom and his wealth, and she praised God for blessing Solomon with such great gifts.

Solomon's Downfall

Solomon's many wives and concubines had a significant impact on his reign. As previously mentioned, some of his wives worshipped foreign gods, which led to Solomon worshipping them as well. This angered God, who warned

Solomon that his actions would lead to the downfall of his kingdom.

Solomon's wives also caused political problems. They brought their own cultures and religions with them, which often conflicted with the customs and beliefs of Israel. This led to tension and division within the kingdom, which would eventually lead to its downfall.

Despite his great wisdom and wealth, Solomon's wives and concubines influenced him in ways that were extremely indicative of the boredom he must have endured being the wisest in the kingdom. They led him astray from his faith and caused him to worship foreign gods as well, which greatly displeased The Highest.

Solomon's relationship with his many wives was complicated. On the one hand, he enjoyed the company of his wives and concubines and is said to have loved many of them deeply. However, he also struggled to maintain control over them, as some of them were known to worship foreign gods and practice rituals that were not in line with Israelite tradition. Attempting to please all of those women was something Solomon sought to do, however, it doesn't seem to have worked out in his favor overall. He agreed to follow after his women, which no one can deny. He also gave himself over to their advice and customs, purposefully forsaking the customs of his people.

This caused problems for Solomon both personally and politically. As he began to adopt the religious practices of his wives, he became increasingly distant from God, who warned him that his actions would lead to the downfall of his kingdom. This prophecy would later come true, as the northern tribes of Israel rebelled against Solomon's son, Rehoboam, and formed the separate Kingdom of Israel.

The Impact of Solomon's Wives

With all of the problems these foreign women caused, Solomon's wives also brought wealth and prosperity to Israel. They brought with them many resources and talents, which were used to build the Temple in Jerusalem and other great works. They also played a role in expanding Israel's trade and influence, which helped to make it one of the wealthiest and most powerful nations in the ancient world.

It is important to note that discretion should always be implemented when seeking out a wife. As Hebrew Israelites, we must take the commands, statutes, and right rulings of The Most High seriously. This means that you should only marry a Hebrew Israelite woman, especially if you want to build a family legacy while avoiding many of the pitfalls that Solomon faced in his life.

Despite the controversies surrounding Solomon's many wives, they left a lasting impact on Israel's history. Many of his wives and concubines went on to play important roles in the history of Israel, both during Solomon's reign and afterward.

Solomon is remembered as one of the greatest kings in the history of Israel. He was known for his wisdom, wealth, and his many achievements, including the building of the Temple in Jerusalem. However, his many wives and their influence on his reign have also been a source of controversy and criticism.

One lesson that can be learned from the story of Solomon and his wives is the danger of forsaking the commands of The Highest in favor of lustful desires.

Another lesson from Solomon's life is the importance of seeking wisdom and understanding. In the Book of Proverbs, Solomon writes about the value of wisdom and knowledge, urging readers to seek them above all else. He also warns against folly and the dangers of living without wisdom, cautioning that it leads to destruction and ruin.

Solomon's Legacy and Lessons Learned

Despite his many accomplishments, Solomon's legacy is not without its lessons. One of the most famous stories about Solomon concerns two women who came to him with a baby, each claiming to be the child's mother. Solomon proposed cutting the baby in half, with each woman receiving an equal portion. The true mother begged Solomon to spare the child and give it to the other woman, revealing her love and selflessness. Solomon awarded the child to the true mother, recognizing her maternal instincts and compassion.

This story is often used as an example of Solomon's wisdom and justice, but it also highlights the importance of empathy and compassion in making difficult decisions. Solomon's reputation for wisdom and wealth often overshadowed his flaws, such as his many wives and concubines, which led to his downfall. According to the Bible, Solomon's idolatry and disobedience to God led to the division of Israel after his death.

The Mighty Queen of Sheba

The Queen of Sheba, also known as the Queen of Saba, is a figure from ancient history and mythology who has captured the imagination of people for centuries. According to the Bible, she visited King Solomon in Jerusalem and was impressed by his wisdom, wealth, and accomplishments. But who was the Queen of Sheba, and what do we know about her?

Origins of the Queen of Sheba

The Queen of Sheba is first mentioned in the Bible in the Book of Kings, which describes her journey to visit King Solomon. The exact location of Sheba is unknown, but it is generally believed to be somewhere in the region of modern-day Ethiopia or Yemen. She is also mentioned in the Quran and Ethiopian and Yemeni folklore.

Historians and scholars have debated the existence of the Queen of Sheba, with some believing she was a real historical figure and others considering her a legendary figure. However, there is evidence of a powerful queen ruling over the ancient kingdom of Saba in southern Arabia, which is believed to have had strong trade connections with Ethiopia.

Who was the Queen of Sheba?

The Queen of Sheba is often depicted as a powerful and intelligent ruler who was fascinated by King Solomon's wisdom and wealth. She is said to have brought him gifts of gold, spices, and precious stones, and engaged in a series of philosophical debates with him. Some accounts suggest that they may have had a romantic relationship, although this is not mentioned in the Bible.

In Ethiopian and Yemeni folklore, the Queen of Sheba is known as Makeda and is said to have been a queen in her own right, ruling over a powerful kingdom. She is often depicted as a wise and just ruler, who was respected by her people for her intelligence and leadership.

Legacy of the Queen of Sheba

The Queen of Sheba has become a symbol of female power and leadership, inspiring stories, songs, and legends throughout history. She is also associated with wealth and prosperity, and her visit to King Solomon has been the subject of many artistic depictions, including paintings, sculptures, and operas.

In Ethiopia, the Queen of Sheba is a revered figure, and her legacy is celebrated in the Ethiopian Orthodox Church, where she is considered a saint. Her story has also been used to promote women's education and empowerment, with many schools and organizations named in her honor.

The Queen of Sheba remains a fascinating and enigmatic figure, whose legacy has captured the imagination of people for centuries. Whether she was a real historical figure or a legendary queen, her story has inspired countless stories, legends, and works of art, and continues to be celebrated today as a symbol of female leadership and empowerment.

Concubines, But Why?

Concubines were women who were in a secondary position to a man's primary wife or wives. In ancient times, including during King Solomon's rule of Israel, it was common for men of wealth and power to have multiple wives and concubines.

While a man's primary wife held a higher status and enjoyed legal and social recognition as his spouse, concubines were generally regarded as inferior to the primary wife and did not enjoy the same legal rights or social status. Concubines were often acquired through various means, such as by purchase, as a gift, or through capture in war, and were typically treated as property.

While concubines were often not as well-off as primary wives, they were generally provided for and had some degree of protection under the law. They were typically housed in separate quarters from the primary wife or wives and their children, and their children did not have the same inheritance rights as the children of the primary wife.

King Solomon's decision to have concubines during his rule of Israel is a complex issue that has been debated by scholars and historians for centuries. While the Bible and other historical texts provide some insight into Solomon's motivations, it is still unclear why he chose to have so many wives and concubines.

One possible explanation for Solomon's decision to have concubines is political. In ancient times, it was common for kings and rulers to form alliances through marriage, and having many wives and concubines could help secure these alliances. It is possible that Solomon used his many marriages to strengthen his position as king and expand his kingdom.

Another possible explanation is religion. According to the Bible, Solomon's many wives and concubines were from different nations and religions, and they introduced foreign gods and practices into Israel. It is possible that Solomon saw these marriages as a way to promote religious tolerance and understanding or to demonstrate his power over other nations and religions.

Some scholars have also suggested that Solomon's many marriages and concubines were a reflection of his wealth and power. In ancient times, having many wives and concubines was a sign of status and wealth, and it is possible that Solomon saw these relationships as a way to demonstrate his wealth and power to others.

However, it is also important to note that Solomon's decision to have many wives and concubines was not without consequences. According to the Bible, his many marriages and concubines led him to worship other gods, which was seen as a grave sin in Israelite culture. His idolatry and disobedience to God are said to have led to the division of Israel after his death.

While we may never know the true motivations behind Solomon's decision to have concubines, it is clear that his actions had both political and religious implications. While some may see his many marriages as a reflection of his power and wealth, others view them as a warning against the dangers of idolatry and the importance of staying true to one's faith.

Honoring The Commitments You Agree To

Solomon's legacy is complex and multifaceted, reflecting the strengths and weaknesses of his character. His wisdom, wealth, and accomplishments are widely admired, but his flaws and mistakes also serve as cautionary tales.

Ultimately, Solomon's legacy reminds us of the importance of seeking wisdom, justice, and compassion in our own lives and leadership.

Honoring commitments is an important aspect of building trust and maintaining healthy relationships, whether they are personal or professional. Solomon began his rule honoring his commitments to The Highest, but the longer he ruled, the farther away from The Most High he found himself.

When you consistently honor the commitments you agree to, your family is more likely to appreciate you in the following ways; here are some best practices to consider when it comes to honoring commitments:

1. **Be realistic:** When you commit, make sure it is achievable and realistic. Consider your time, resources, and other commitments before making promises. Be honest with yourself and others about what you can and cannot do.

2. **Communicate clearly:** When making commitments, be clear about what you are agreeing to do. This includes the scope, timeline, and expectations. If there are any changes or challenges, communicate them as soon as possible to avoid surprises and misunderstandings.

3. **Prioritize commitments:** Make sure you prioritize your commitments and follow through on the most important ones first. This helps ensure that you are meeting your obligations and delivering on your promises.

4. **Take ownership:** If you are unable to fulfill a commitment, take ownership of it and communicate it as soon as possible. Offer alternative solutions or make arrangements to fulfill the commitment at a later time.

5. **Plan:** Planning can help you avoid over-committing and ensure that you have the time and resources to meet your commitments. Create a schedule or calendar and stick to it as much as possible.

6. **Review regularly:** Review your commitments regularly to ensure that you are on track and meeting your obligations. This helps you stay accountable and make adjustments as needed.

7. **Learn from mistakes:** If you do fail to honor a commitment, take the opportunity to learn from it. Identify what went wrong and what you can do differently in the future to avoid making the same mistake.

8. **Trust and respect:** When you consistently follow through on your commitments, your family members will trust and respect you more. They will know that they can rely on you to do what you say you will do, which builds a strong foundation of trust and respect in your relationships.

9. **Open communication:** Honoring commitments requires open communication, which is an essential element of healthy relationships. When you communicate clearly and honestly about your commitments,

your family will appreciate your transparency and the fact that you are willing to be accountable for your actions.

10. **Positive impact:** When you honor your commitments, you are more likely to have a positive impact on your family. You may be more available to help out with tasks and activities, or you may be more willing to listen to their needs and concerns. This can help build a stronger sense of family unity and support.

11. **Role modeling:** By honoring your commitments, you are setting a positive example for your family members. They will see that you value integrity, responsibility, and accountability, and they may be more likely to adopt these qualities themselves.

12. **Appreciation and gratitude:** When you consistently follow through on your commitments, your family members are more likely to appreciate and express gratitude for your efforts. They may recognize the time, energy, and sacrifice that you put into fulfilling your commitments, and they may be more willing to reciprocate when you need their help in the future.

By following these best practices, you can honor the commitments you agree to and build strong, trustworthy relationships with those around you. Honoring commitments is an important way to build healthy relationships with your family.

When you consistently follow through on your commitments, you will earn their trust and respect, set a positive example, and create a more positive and supportive family environment.

6

THE STORY OF GIDEON AND HIS MANY WIVES

The Biblical story of Gideon and his many wives is found in the book of Judges, chapters 6-8. Gideon was a judge of Israel, chosen by God to lead the Israelites in the battle against the Midianites.

In Judges 6, we learn that the Israelites had been oppressed by the Midianites for seven years. God called upon Gideon to lead the Israelites in the battle against the Midianites, and Gideon was initially hesitant, questioning why God had chosen him for such a task.

The Most High promised to be with Gideon and to give him victory over the Midianites. Gideon asked for a sign of God's favor, and God performed a miracle by burning up a sacrifice that Gideon had offered on a rock.

Gideon then gathered an army of 32,000 men to fight the Midianites. But God instructed Gideon to reduce the size of his army, saying that the Israelites would take credit for the victory if they won with such a large army. Gideon obeyed God and sent home all but 300 of his men.

With this small band of soldiers, Gideon attacked the Midianite camp in the middle of the night, surprising and confusing the enemy. The Midianites fled, and Gideon and his men pursued them, eventually defeating them.

After the victory, Gideon was asked to be king of Israel, but he refused, saying that God was the only true king. However, Gideon did ask for payment for his service, and he collected gold earrings from the defeated Midianites, which he used to make a golden ephod, a religious garment.

Unfortunately, this victory did not bring lasting peace to Israel. Gideon, who had many wives and concubines, had a son named Abimelech by one of his concubines. Abimelech went on to murder his half-brothers and become king of Israel, leading to a time of strife and chaos.

After Gideon's death, his son Abimelech went to Shechem, where he convinced his mother's people to make him their king. Abimelech had already murdered his brothers, who were also sons of Gideon, to eliminate any competition for the throne.

However, Abimelech's rule was short-lived and marked by violence and chaos. He killed many of his people and waged war against the nearby city of Thebez. During the battle, a woman dropped a millstone on Abimelech's head, mortally wounding him.

The narrative concerning Abimelech serves as a cautionary tale about the dangers of ambition, violence, and the pursuit of power. It also highlights the consequences of Gideon's actions in having many wives and concubines, as it led to a complex and divided family dynamic that ultimately contributed to the downfall of his son.

Overall, the story of Gideon is one of God's faithfulness and provision, even in the face of overwhelming odds. However, it also highlights the dangers of pride and disobedience, as seen in the later actions of Gideon's son Abimelech.

How Do We View Ourselves In The Face Of Adversity?

Gideon is one of the most prominent figures in the Old Testament of the Bible. He is known for his unwavering faith in God and his ability to lead his people to victory in the face of overwhelming odds. Throughout his life, Gideon faced many challenges and obstacles, but he never lost sight of his purpose and his faith in God.

One of the most striking examples of Gideon's resilience in the face of adversity is his response to God's call to lead the Israelites against the Midianites. When God first approached Gideon with this task, Gideon was hesitant and full of self-doubt. He saw himself as a weak and insignificant member of his tribe, and he couldn't understand why God would choose him for such an important task.

But despite his initial reluctance, Gideon eventually accepted God's call and set out to lead the Israelites into battle. Along the way, he faced many challenges and setbacks, including a lack of resources, an overwhelming enemy force, and the betrayal of his people. But even in the face of these obstacles, Gideon never lost his faith in God or his commitment to his mission.

One of the most powerful examples of Gideon's faith and determination comes from his battle against the Midianites. Despite being vastly outnumbered, Gideon and his small army were able to defeat the Midianites by relying on God's guidance and strength. Gideon's unwavering faith in God's power and his willingness to follow God's lead were the key factors that led to his victory.

Throughout his life, Gideon faced many challenges and obstacles, but he always saw himself as a faithful servant of God, worthy of God's love and protection. He never lost sight of his purpose or his faith, and he remained steadfast in the face of adversity. In the end, Gideon's story serves as a powerful example of what can be accomplished when one trusts in God's power and follows his guidance.

Adversity is an inevitable part of life. At some point, we will all face challenges and obstacles that test our strength, resilience, and character. How we view ourselves in the face of adversity can have a profound impact on our ability to overcome these challenges and emerge stronger on the other side.

One of the key factors that determine how we view ourselves in the face of adversity is our mindset. Those with a growth mindset tend to view challenges as opportunities for learning and growth, while those with a fixed mindset tend to view challenges as threats to their abilities and self-worth.

When we face adversity, it is natural to experience a range of emotions, including fear, doubt, and frustration. However, it is important to remember that these emotions do not define us. We can choose to see ourselves as strong, capable, and resilient, even in the face of our greatest challenges.

One way to cultivate a positive self-view in the face of adversity is to focus on our strengths and accomplishments. Reflecting on our past successes can help us build confidence and resilience, and give us the strength we need to face new challenges.

Another key factor in how we view ourselves in the face of adversity is the support of those around us. Having a strong support system can help us stay grounded, provide encouragement and motivation, and remind us of our inherent value and worth.

It is also important to remember that adversity is not a reflection of our worth as individuals. We are all capable of facing challenges and overcoming them, and our struggles do not define us. Instead, they can be opportunities for growth, learning, and personal transformation.

In the face of adversity, it can be easy to lose sight of our strengths, abilities, and self-worth. But by cultivating a positive mindset, focusing on our past successes, seeking the support of others, and remembering our inherent value, we can view ourselves as strong, capable, and resilient, and face our challenges with confidence and courage.

When facing adversity, it is important to adopt healthy and effective practices for viewing ourselves in a positive light.

Here are some best practices for cultivating a positive self-view in the face of adversity:

1. **Develop a growth mindset:** A growth mindset is a belief that our abilities and intelligence can be developed through hard work, dedication, and persistence. This mindset helps us see adversity as an opportunity for growth and learning, rather than a threat to our self-worth. Adopting a growth mindset can help us view ourselves as capable and resilient in the face of challenges.
2. **Practice self-compassion:** Self-compassion involves treating ourselves with kindness, understanding, and acceptance, especially in times of difficulty. This means recognizing that we are human and imperfect and that we all experience challenges and setbacks. Practicing self-compassion can help us view ourselves in a more positive light and build resilience in the face of adversity.
3. **Focus on our strengths and accomplishments:** Reflecting on our past successes and strengths can help us build confidence and self-esteem. This can include acknowledging our skills, accomplishments, and personal qualities. By focusing on our strengths, we can cultivate a positive self-view that can help us face adversity with greater resilience.

4. **Seek social support:** Having a supportive network of family, friends, or peers can provide emotional support and encouragement when facing adversity. This can include seeking guidance, feedback, or encouragement from others. Social support can help us feel valued and supported and can contribute to a more positive self-view.

5. **Challenge negative self-talk:** Negative self-talk can be a major obstacle to a positive self-view. It is important to challenge negative self-talk by recognizing and disputing negative beliefs or assumptions. This can involve reframing negative thoughts into more positive and realistic statements or seeking out evidence that contradicts negative self-beliefs.

Establishing an expanded family is not for the faint of heart. As men, we can learn from Gideon's experiences in many ways. There were moments when Gideon had the odds stacked against him, but he persevered by remembering his "why".

When we are building our family, we must have our "why" in clear focus. Our "why" is the deep-seated reason that we hold close to our hearts, which cannot be abandoned, regardless of the situation or odds stacked against us on our way to achieving the goals that we set for ourselves.

By adopting these best practices, we can cultivate a positive self-view in the face of adversity. These practices can help us build resilience, develop a growth mindset, and foster self-compassion, which can contribute to greater well-being and success in the face of challenges.

7

THE STORY OF ABIJAH AND HIS FOURTEEN WIVES

Who Was Abijah?

The story of Abijah and his fourteen wives is a narrative found in the Bible, specifically in 2 Chronicles 13:21. Abijah was the son of King Rehoboam and the grandson of King Solomon. He became the king of Judah after his father's death and ruled for three years.

The story goes that Abijah had fourteen wives, and he fathered twenty-two sons and sixteen daughters with them, making a total of thirty-eight children altogether. The Most High blessed him for being a righteous man and multiplying the children of Israel. What a blessed man to be able to have so many devoted wives and children!

The Bible describes Abijah as a righteous king who did what was pleasing in the eyes of The Highest. He fought a successful battle against Jeroboam, the king of Israel, who had twice as many soldiers as Abijah did. The battle was won because Abijah relied on God's help and guidance.

However, after the battle, Abijah fell ill and eventually died. The Bible does not provide any details on how his wives and children were affected by his death or how they continued to live their lives after he passed away.

The story of Abijah is one of deep faith and adherence to God's laws. Abijah was a righteous king, whose actions regarding his many wives helped solidify his family legacy and ensured that the Divine lineage he carried would continue into future generations after his death. His having multiple wives did not lead to his eventual demise, as some Western scholars would like to suggest, but instead ensured that his progeny would live on well after he had transitioned from this realm.

The story of Abijah serves as a reminder that even the most righteous of individuals will one day pass on, and that there must be a system in place about an individual's Divine Family Unit for when that time comes. It also serves as a reminder of the fleeting nature of life and the importance of living by God's commands.

Abijah Declares Battle

Abijah and Jeroboam fought in battle against one another because of a long-standing feud between the kingdoms of Judah and Israel.

After the reign of King Solomon, the united kingdom of Israel split into two separate kingdoms: Israel in the north and Judah in the south. Jeroboam was the king of Israel, and Abijah was the king of Judah. According to the Bible, the two kingdoms had been at odds with each other for many years.

In particular, the conflict between Abijah and Jeroboam arose when Jeroboam led a rebellion against King Rehoboam, Abijah's father, and took control of ten of the tribes of Israel, leaving only two tribes under the rule of Rehoboam's descendants in Judah. This division caused ongoing tension and conflict between the two kingdoms.

When Abijah became king, he was determined to reclaim the ten tribes that had been taken by Jeroboam. He assembled an army of 400,000 men, while Jeroboam's army consisted of 800,000 soldiers. Despite being outnumbered, Abijah believed that God was on his side and that he would be victorious in battle.

The battle between Abijah and Jeroboam took place at Mount Zemaraim, in the hill country of Ephraim. Abijah gave a rousing speech to his troops, reminding them that God had given the kingdom of Israel to David and his descendants forever. He also pointed out that Jeroboam and his people were worshiping false gods, while the people of Judah remained faithful to the one true God.

In the end, Abijah's faith in God proved justified, as Judah emerged victorious in battle, killing 500,000 soldiers from Israel. The conflict between the two kingdoms continued, however, and the Bible records several more battles between Judah and Israel over the years.

In summary, Abijah and Jeroboam fought in the battle against one another due to the long-standing feud between the kingdoms of Israel and Judah, and specifically, because of Jeroboam's rebellion against Abijah's father and his taking control of ten of the tribes of Israel. Abijah believed that God was on his side and that he would be victorious in battle, and ultimately, Judah emerged victorious, though the conflict between the two kingdoms continued.

Abijah Teaches Us A Great Lesson

Abijah, the righteous king of Judah, whose rule was powerful, but extremely short-lived, taught us many lessons about dedication, the will to survive, belief in God, faith in God, and leaving a lasting legacy. If we take a careful look at the narrative surrounding him, we will be wise to take into account his unwavering faith in The Most High, and how his faith helped him become victorious over his foes. His enemies were, unfortunately, his kinsman.

Many sons of Israel were killed on both sides of the great conflict, and we have to ask ourselves a serious question: what types of provisions and planning were in place for all of these men who surely had wives and children expecting them to return from the battle, but who didn't make it home?

Establishing safeguards for our family in case of an untimely demise is a wise and responsible thing to do. While thinking about our mortality is never easy, taking steps to protect our loved ones can provide peace of mind and ensure that they are taken care of in our absence.

Here are some important steps and best practices you can take to establish safeguards for your family in case of an untimely demise:

1. **Write a Will:** A will is a legal document that outlines your wishes for how your assets should be distributed after your death. This ensures that your assets are distributed according to your wishes and can help prevent any family disputes that might arise. It is important to update your will regularly as your life circumstances change. You should consult with a lawyer to ensure that your will is valid and up to date.

2. **Designate a Guardian for Your Children:** If you have minor

children, it is important to designate a guardian in your will who will take care of them in the event of your untimely demise. It is important to choose someone you trust and who shares your values and beliefs. Your wives will be instrumental in raising your children under the principles you've instilled into your Divine Family Unit in case of an untimely demise, so make sure you are clear and concise when you voice your instructions to them regarding this very important topic of discussion. This can be done through your will or a separate document.

3. **Create a Trust:** A trust is a legal arrangement in which you transfer ownership of your assets to a trustee who will manage them on behalf of your beneficiaries. This can help ensure that your assets are used to provide for your family according to your wishes. Trusts can be complex legal documents, so it's important to consult with a lawyer.

4. **Purchase Life Insurance:** Life insurance can provide financial support to your family in the event of your untimely death. It can help cover expenses such as funeral costs, outstanding debts, and ongoing living expenses. Consult with a financial advisor to determine the amount of coverage you need. You can also create streams of revenue that can be accrued daily, even while you sleep. These ventures will pay dividends to you and your family later, as long you consistently tend to them and save your incoming profits correctly.

5. **Organize Your Financial and Legal Documents:** It is important to keep your financial and legal documents organized and easily accessible to your loved ones. This includes your will, life insurance policies, bank account information, and other important documents.

6. **Communicate Your Wishes:** It is important to communicate your wishes to your loved ones so they are aware of your plans and can carry them out accordingly. This can help prevent any confusion or misunderstandings that might arise after your death.

Establishing safeguards for your family in case of an untimely demise is a responsible way to protect your loved ones and provide for them in the event of your death. By taking these steps, you can have peace of mind knowing that your family will be taken care of according to your wishes.

Abijah's story teaches us the importance of holding onto our faith, even in the face of adversity. Abijah was confronted with a difficult situation when his kinsman Jeroboam declared war on him. Jeroboam had twice as many soldiers as Abijah did, but Abijah did not despair. Instead, he relied on God's help and guidance to lead him to victory.

Abijah's faith in God was not only evident in his military strategy, but also his personal life. Abijah was described as a righteous king with fourteen wives, who did what was pleasing in the eyes of The Most High. This shows that even when we choose to live a life contrary to what modern society thinks if we live according to the laws, statutes, commands, and right rulings of The Most High, we will be rewarded and blessed for our service and faith in Him.

Another lesson we can learn from Abijah's story is the importance of leaving a lasting legacy. Despite ruling for only three years, Abijah's legacy lived on through his sons and daughters. He had a large family and was able to pass on his faith and values to them. This serves as a reminder that we should strive to leave a positive impact on those around us, whether it be our family or our community.

Abijah's story teaches us about the power of faith, the importance of forgiveness, and the significance of leaving a lasting legacy. By following in Abijah's footsteps, we can strive to be righteous individuals who are dedicated to God, our families, and our communities.

8

THE STORY OF ELKANAH AND HIS MANY WIVES

Who Was Elkanah?

The biblical story of Elkanah and his many wives is found in the Old Testament book of 1 Samuel, specifically in chapters 1 and 2. Elkanah was a man from the tribe of Ephraim who lived during the time of the judges in Israel. He had two wives, Peninnah, and Hannah.

The story begins with Elkanah going up to the Tabernacle in Shiloh to worship and make sacrifices to the Lord. During one of these visits, Elkanah gave portions of the sacrificial meat to each of his wives, but he gave a double portion to Hannah because he loved her more, even though she was barren.

Peninnah, who had many children, would often provoke and taunt Hannah because of her barrenness, causing her great distress. Despite this, Elkanah would try to comfort Hannah and reassure her of his love.

One year, when Elkanah and his family went up to the Tabernacle to worship, Hannah went into the temple to pray. In her desperation, she wept and poured out her heart to The Most High, promising to dedicate any child she had to Him. The priest Eli, who was watching her, initially thought she was drunk, but upon realizing her sincerity, blessed her and prayed that her request would be granted.

The Most High answered Hannah's prayer and she conceived and gave birth to a son, whom she named Samuel. As she had promised, Hannah dedicated Samuel to The Highest and brought him to the Tabernacle to serve under the priest Eli.

In Chapter 2, Hannah praises God for answering her prayer and giving her a child. She also acknowledges that God is a God of justice and that He will bring low those who exalt themselves and raise the humble.

The story of Elkanah and his many wives highlights the cultural practices of our fore-parents, where it has always been acceptable for men to have multiple wives. However, it also shows the pain and jealousy that can arise in such situations. The story also emphasizes the power of prayer and the faithfulness of God in answering the prayers of His people.

Who Was Peninnah?

The story of Peninnah, the wife of Elkanah, is found in the Old Testament book of 1 Samuel, primarily in chapters 1 and 2. Peninnah was one of Elkanah's wives and the mother of several children, while Elkanah's other wife, Hannah, was barren and childless.

Peninnah is portrayed as a woman who took advantage of her position as a mother and taunted Hannah because she was unable to have children. The Bible says that Peninnah would provoke and irritate Hannah until she wept and would not eat. This went on year after year, and it was a source of great pain and distress for Hannah.

It is not clear why Peninnah acted in this way. Perhaps she was jealous of the love and attention that Elkanah showed to Hannah, or perhaps she was simply a cruel and malicious person. Whatever the reason, her behavior towards Hannah was cruel and hurtful.

Despite Peninnah's taunts, Hannah did not retaliate or seek revenge. Instead, she turned to The Highest in prayer and poured out her heart to Him. She asked God to give her a child, promising to dedicate the child to Him if He granted her request.

The Most High answered Hannah's prayer, and she gave birth to a son, whom she named Samuel. She kept her promise and dedicated Samuel to The Highest, bringing him to the temple to serve under the priest Eli.

After Samuel was born, Peninnah's taunts and insults toward Hannah ceased. It is not clear why this happened, but it is possible that Peninnah realized the error of her ways and the pain that she had caused Hannah.

The story of Peninnah highlights the importance of treating others with kindness and compassion, even in difficult circumstances. It also shows the power of prayer and the faithfulness of God in answering the prayers of His people.

Ultimately, Peninnah's role in the story serves as a reminder that we should always strive to treat others with love and respect, even when we may not understand their circumstances.

Who Was Hannah?

The biblical story of Hannah, the wife of Elkanah, is found in the Old Testament book of 1 Samuel, specifically in chapters 1 and 2. Hannah is a woman who longs for a child but is unable to conceive. Her story is a testament to the power of prayer and the faithfulness of God.

Hannah was one of Elkanah's wives, but unlike his other wife, Peninnah, Hannah was barren and unable to have children. This was a source of great pain and shame for Hannah, as having children was highly valued in ancient Israelite culture.

Despite her barrenness, Hannah never lost faith in God. Year after year, she would go with her family to the Tabernacle in Shiloh to worship and make offerings to The Most High. On one such occasion, Hannah was so distraught and overwhelmed with sadness that she poured out her heart to God in prayer. She vowed to dedicate any child that God would give her to His service.

Eli, the priest who was serving at the Tabernacle, saw Hannah praying silently and assumed she was drunk. When Hannah explained her situation to him, Eli blessed her and prayed for her, assuring her that God would grant her request. Hannah left the tabernacle feeling hopeful and encouraged.

The Most High answered Hannah's prayer, and she conceived and gave birth to a son, whom she named Samuel. True to her vow, she brought Samuel to the Tabernacle in Shiloh when he was weaned and presented him to Eli to serve in The Most High's house.

Hannah's prayer of thanksgiving and praise, which is recorded in 1 Samuel 2, is a beautiful testament to her faith in God and her recognition of His sovereignty and goodness. In it, she praises God for His faithfulness, His power and majesty, and His provision of her son Samuel.

Hannah's story is a powerful reminder that God is faithful and answers the prayers of His people. It also illustrates the importance of perseverance and faith, even in the face of great trials and challenges. Finally, it highlights the power of a mother's love and sacrifice, as Hannah was willing to give up her only son to serve The Most High's purposes.

Hannah's prayer of thanksgiving and praise is recorded in 1 Samuel 2:1-10. It is a beautiful and powerful prayer that expresses her gratitude and joy for God's faithfulness and provision, as well as her trust in His sovereignty and power.

Here is the text of her prayer: YaHeWaHe

"My heart rejoices in YaHeWaHe;
　　in YaHeWaHe my horn is lifted high.
　　My mouth boasts over my enemies,
　　for I delight in your deliverance.
　　"There is no one holy like YaHeWaHe;
　　there is no one besides you;
　　there is no Rock like our God.

"Do not keep talking so proudly
　　or let your mouth speak such arrogance,
　　for YaHeWaHe is a God who knows,
　　and by Him, deeds are weighed.

"The bows of the warriors are broken,
　　but those who stumbled are armed with strength.
　　Those who were full hire themselves out for food,
　　but those who were hungry are hungry no more.
　　She who was barren has borne seven children,

but she who has had many sons pines away.
"YaHeWaHe brings death and makes alive;
He brings down to the grave and raises up.
YaHeWaHe sends poverty and wealth;
He humbles and He exalts.
He raises the poor from the dust
and lifts the needy from the ash heap;
He seats them with princes
and has them inherit a throne of honor.
"For the foundations of the earth are YaHeWaIIe's;
on them, He has set the world.
He will guard the feet of His faithful servants,
but the wicked will be silenced in the place of darkness.
"It is not by strength that one prevails;
those who oppose YaHeWaHe will be broken.
The Highest will thunder from heaven;
YaHeWaHe will judge the ends of the earth.
"He will give strength to His king
and exalt the horn of His anointed."

Let us all give praise! What a mighty and beautiful prayer indeed!

Who Was Samuel?

The biblical story of Samuel, the son of Elkanah and Hannah, is found in the Old Testament book of 1 Samuel. Samuel is one of the most important figures in Israelite history, as he was the last of the judges and the first of the prophets. His story is a powerful example of faithfulness and obedience to God.

Samuel was born to Hannah, who had been barren after she had prayed to God for a child. In gratitude for God's gift of a son, Hannah dedicated Samuel to The Most High's service from his earliest days. She brought him to the Tabernacle in Shiloh when he was weaned and left him there with the priest Eli so that he might serve in the house of YaHeWaHe.

As Samuel grew up, he proved to be a faithful and obedient servant of God. He ministered to Eli and assisted in the Tabernacle, and he was known throughout Israel as a prophet and judge. One of Samuel's most important roles was to anoint Saul as the first king of Israel, at God's command. Later, Samuel also anointed David as king, by God's plan.

Throughout his life, Samuel was a faithful servant of God, who put his trust in Him above all else. He listened carefully to God's voice and obeyed His commands, even when they were difficult or unpopular. He warned the Israelites of the dangers of turning away from God and encouraged them to seek His guidance and protection.

In his old age, Samuel continued to serve God and the people of Israel faithfully. He called them to repentance and urged them to remain faithful to The Most High, even as he knew that his own time on earth was drawing to a close. When Samuel died, he was mourned by all Israel, as a true servant of God and a wise and just judge.

The story of Samuel is a powerful reminder of the importance of faithfulness and obedience to God. It teaches us to listen carefully to God's voice and to trust in His wisdom and guidance. Samuel's life is a testament to the power of God to use even the most unlikely and humble servants for His purposes, and to the importance of living a life of integrity and faithfulness in all that we do.

How To Avoid Jealousy, Even Though We Have All That We Desire

Jealousy is a natural human emotion that can arise when we perceive that others have something that we lack or desire. However, jealousy can be destructive and lead to negative feelings and behaviors, such as resentment, anger, and even aggression.

Jealousy is also a natural emotion that can arise in any relationship, including marriage. However, if left unchecked, jealousy can lead to distrust, conflict, and even the breakdown of the relationship. Here are some tips, or best practices to help avoid jealousy as a wife:

1. **Focus on what you have:** Instead of focusing on what others have, focus on the blessings and accomplishments in your own life. Practice gratitude and take time to appreciate the things you have, such as your health, family, and friends.
2. **Cultivate compassion:** Try to understand the other person's perspective and circumstances, and cultivate empathy and compassion towards them. Recognize that everyone has their challenges and struggles and that their success or good fortune does not diminish your own.
3. **Avoid comparison:** Avoid comparing yourself to others, especially on social media, which can often create unrealistic expectations and lead to feelings of inadequacy. Instead, focus on your journey and progress, and celebrate your accomplishments and milestones.
4. **Develop self-confidence:** One of the main reasons for jealousy is a lack of self-confidence. Work on developing your self-confidence and self-worth, so that you are not dependent on external validation or comparison to others. Practice self-care, positive self-talk, and engage in activities that make you feel good about yourself. Focus on your strengths and accomplishments and avoid comparing yourself to

others. Recognize that you are truly unique and valuable.

5. **Reframe the situation:** Instead of seeing the other person as a threat or competitor, reframe the situation as an opportunity to learn and grow. Seek inspiration and motivation from their success, and use it as a catalyst to drive your progress and achievement.

6. **Trust your husband:** Trust is the foundation of any successful relationship. Trust that your husband loves and cares for you and that he is committed to the relationship. If you have concerns or doubts, talk to your husband about them calmly and openly.

7. **Communicate openly:** Communication is key to any successful relationship. Be open and honest with your husband about your feelings and concerns. Avoid making assumptions or jumping to conclusions without having all the facts.

8. **Focus on the positive:** Instead of dwelling on negative thoughts or feelings, focus on the positive aspects of your relationship. Celebrate your successes and accomplishments together and show gratitude for each other's support.

9. **Spend time together:** Make time to connect with your husband regularly. Plan fun activities, go on dates, or simply spend time relaxing together. By focusing on building a strong and healthy relationship, you can reduce feelings of jealousy.

10. **Seek help if needed:** If you find that jealousy is becoming a persistent problem, seek help from a therapist or counselor. They can provide support and guidance to help you work through your feelings and improve your relationship.

Jealousy is a natural emotion, but it doesn't have to control your thoughts or actions. By building self-confidence, trusting your husband, communicating openly, focusing on the positive, spending time together, and seeking help if needed, you can avoid jealousy and build a strong and healthy relationship.

Elkanah deserves some recognition too. He was a supportive husband and didn't allow his wife Peninnah to continually taunt and make fun of his wife Hannah. We can learn from his fortitude and actions, especially in our relationships as we grow our Divine Family Unit.

Being a supportive husband to your wife is essential for a strong and healthy relationship. Here are some tips on how to be a supportive husband:

1. **Listen actively:** One of the most important ways to support your wife is to listen actively to her. This means being present and attentive when she is speaking and trying to understand her perspective without judgment.
2. **Show empathy:** Show empathy by trying to understand and share your wife's feelings. Be sensitive to her emotions and offer comfort and support when needed.
3. **Validate her feelings:** Let your wife know that her feelings are valid and that you respect and understand them. This can go a long way in making her feel heard and valued.
4. **Offer practical support:** Help your wife with tasks and responsibilities that she may be struggling with, such as household chores or childcare. This can help to ease her burden and make her feel supported.
5. **Show appreciation:** Show appreciation for your wife's contributions to the relationship and the family. Let her know that you value her and are grateful for all that she does.
6. **Be her partner:** Work with your wife as a team, sharing responsibilities and making decisions together. Show her that you are committed to the relationship and are willing to work through challenges together.
7. **Be patient:** Be patient with your wife when she is going through a difficult time or is facing a challenge. Support her as she works through these challenges and offer her encouragement along the way.

Remember, being a supportive husband is about being present, listening actively, and offering practical and emotional support when needed. By showing empathy, validating her feelings, showing appreciation, working as a team, and being patient, you can be a supportive and loving partner to your wife.

By following these best practices, you can learn to overcome jealousy and cultivate a positive and fulfilling mindset that is focused on your happiness and growth. Remember, success is not a zero-sum game, and there is enough room for everyone to thrive and succeed in their unique way.

9

THE STORY OF HAMASHIACH'S PARABLE OF THE WISE AND FOOLISH VIRGINS

One Parable That Is Not What It Seems At First Glance

The parable of the wise and foolish virgins, or maidens, is a story told by YaHeWaShA HaMashiach in the New Testament of the Bible. It is found in the Gospel of Matthew, chapter 25, verses 1-13. The parable is about ten virgins who are waiting for a bridegroom to arrive so they can attend a wedding feast together.

Before we continue, it is important to know the definition of a bridegroom. A bridegroom is a man who is about to be married, or who has just been married.

Now that we are clear on the definition of a bridegroom, what is a maiden, and what is a virgin? A maiden is an old-fashioned term for a girl or an unmarried young woman, while a virgin is a person who has never had sexual intercourse.

In the parable, five of the virgins are described as wise and five are described as foolish. The wise virgins brought extra oil for their lamps, while the foolish virgins did not. When the bridegroom was delayed, all of the virgins fell asleep. But when the bridegroom finally arrived, the wise virgins were able to light their lamps and join him at the wedding feast, while the foolish virgins were left outside in the dark.

Many people who have read or heard this story of the Ten Wise and Foolish Virgins don't realize the connotations of it. The ten virgins, or maidens, referred to in the parable, were waiting for the bridegroom because they were going to be entering into a marital union with him. That's right: these young women were to be married to the bridegroom they were waiting for.

We can deduce this conclusion because maidens do not wait for a bridegroom; they tend to and await the bride. In the parable, the maidens are waiting to enter the wedding feast because they are to be married to the bridegroom, who has tarried his arrival to separate those wise and frugal maidens from the foolish ones.

The spiritual meaning of the parable is that we Israelites should always be prepared for the coming of HaMashiach because we do not know when it will happen. The wise virgins represent those who are ready and prepared for HaMashiach's return, while the foolish virgins represent those who are not prepared and will be left behind.

The extra oil that the wise virgins brought represents the spiritual preparedness that we need to have to be ready for HaMashiach's return. We must always be growing in our faith, seeking to know God more deeply, and living in a way that is pleasing to Him.

The parable also warns us not to rely on the faith of others, but to take responsibility for our own spiritual lives. The foolish virgins assumed that the oil would be shared among them, but they were wrong. We cannot rely on others to give us spiritual preparedness - it is something that we must seek and cultivate for ourselves.

HaMashiach is the bridegroom to the gathering of believers, also known as the "church". The church isn't comprised of just one believer but of many believers. This vast group of believers makes up the body of believers that are in covenant, or marriage, with HaMashiach. This marriage isn't a monogamous one either. This body of believers is comprised of many people who live with HaMashiach as their King and spiritual covering. This is why HaMashiach uses this parable to illustrate this great and important truth.

The ten virgins in the parable are not named, and their identities are not important to the meaning of the story. Rather, they serve as symbols of preparedness and readiness for the coming of HaMashiach. The wise virgins represent those who are ready and prepared for HaMashiach's return, while the foolish virgins represent those who are not prepared and will be left behind.

On the surface, the parable of the wise and foolish virgins reminds and teaches us of the significance of Hebraic marriage culture and the early preparations involved with an expanded family. The exoteric meaning of the parable of the wise and foolish virgins teaches us to be prepared for the coming of HaMashiach, to take responsibility for our spiritual preparedness, and to not rely on the faith of others.

May we all be like the wise virgins, ready and waiting for HaMashiach's return.

A Misunderstood Law That Must Be Clarified

Before we continue, we should discuss a verse that is oftentimes miscon-strued. Many parishioners have referenced Matthew 19:9 to justify their stance on divorce. However, Matthew 19:9 is a verse justifying polygyny while referencing divorce to drive home the validity of polygyny.

Matthew 19:9 is indeed a verse from the Bible that has been subject to different interpretations and understandings. It is important to note that interpretations of Biblical texts can vary among different individuals and religious traditions. In this chapter, we will break the verse down into its simplest form, and analyze it with an unbiased and contextually sound perspective.

In Matthew 19:9, Yahewasha is addressing the issue of divorce and polygyny. He states, "And I say unto you, Whosoever shall put away his wife, except it be for fornication, and shall marry another, committeth adultery: and whoso marrieth her which is put away doth commit adultery."

The verse implies that marrying another woman after divorcing your first wife is generally not permissible, except in cases of marital infidelity, often translated as "adultery" in this context. It is important to understand that adultery refers to sexual immorality.

This verse also implies that if you don't put away your first wife, it is perfectly permissible to marry another woman.

We must keep in mind that the Scriptures are a book of laws, ordinances, and statutes. Assuming that an individual will understand the Bible without a serious amount of study is a gross mistake.

A person couldn't just become a lawyer without extensively studying penal codes and state laws. The same can be said for the laws located within the Bible. Furthermore, this particular set of laws, statutes, and ordinances was given to the children of Israel, the men in particular, by The Most High.

This means that the instructions listed in the Bible must be viewed from a Hebraic perspective and not a Romantic one.

When a married woman has sexual relations with another man (whether he is already married to another woman or not), or when a man (married or non-married) has sexual relations with a married woman, it is referred to as adultery. Many people make a huge mistake when they apply this clause to a man who is already married and has sexual relations with a non-married woman.

To simplify the verse completely: a married man may have sexual relations with a non-married woman, and not be accused of committing adultery. If he doesn't marry her, they would have committed the act of fornication. If he does marry her, there is absolutely nothing wrong with this and they can go on to live a full, and complete married life together.

After these specific prerequisites have been met, joining into a covenant together, and living in the fullness of commitment between one another defines a Biblical marriage.

To understand this verse completely, we must recognize the clauses referenced within it to gain clarity.

One of the first things that we will need to accept is that all adultery is fornication, but all fornication isn't adultery. Let's dissect the verse and take a closer look at what it says.

Matthew 19:9 states:

1. "And I say unto you, whosoever shall put away his wife,

2. except it be for fornication,

3. and shall marry another,

4. committeth adultery:

5. and whoso marrieth her which is put away doth commit adultery."

EXPLANATION

This verse is one of the most understated verses within the Bible that supports our ancient Hebraic practice of polygyny. What we can take away from this one extremely important verse is:

1. Don't put away your wife AND take another wife unless...

2. Unless what? your "first wife" commits adultery (sleeping with another man while she is married to you).

3. If a new man comes along and marries a woman who was married but has been put away due to anything except for that fornication, the new man commits adultery too.

4. Moral of the verse: long-suffer in truth with your wife. Don't be so quick to divorce her for the small things.

5. You are allowed by Biblical law to marry another wife. You are not allowed to marry another wife after putting your first one away if she (the first wife) is not being put away for fornication only. It is permissible to marry another woman while remaining in marriage to your initial wife.

Before moving forward with the remainder of this chapter, it is advised to review this section for clarity. Take your time unpacking the breakdown of Matthew 19:9 and review the verse for yourself. Remember to analyze this verse from a Hebraic perspective and to also refer to the Torah.

Yahewasha came to fulfill the law (Torah), not to break it. He wouldn't suggest for his kinsman to do anything that isn't sound direction according to Torah.

How To Prepare For An Opportunity We've Always Hoped For

Opportunities can arise at any time and in unexpected ways. Sometimes, the opportunity we have always hoped for may come knocking on our door when we least expect it. To be ready for such opportunities, it is important to stay prepared and focused. Here are some tips on how to stay ready for an opportunity we've always hoped for:

1. **Define Your Goals and Be Prepared:** To stay ready for the opportunities we've always hoped for, we need to know what we want to achieve. Defining our goals and outlining the steps we need to take to achieve them can help us stay focused and motivated. We should also be prepared for any situation that may arise in the pursuit of our goals.
2. **Keep Learning and Growing:** Continuous learning and personal growth are important aspects of staying ready for opportunities. We should seek to learn new skills, read books, attend seminars, and engage in activities that can help us grow both personally and professionally. This will increase our knowledge and confidence, making us better

equipped to seize any opportunity that comes our way.

3. **Network and Build Relationships:** Networking and building relationships with people in our field can also help us stay ready for opportunities. We should connect with like-minded people, attend industry events, and join professional associations. By doing so, we can expand our network, learn from others, and increase our chances of being in the right place at the right time.

4. **Stay Positive and Focused:** Staying positive and focused is essential in staying ready for opportunities. We should maintain a positive mindset, visualize our goals, and stay focused on our priorities. This will help us stay motivated and persistent, even in the face of challenges and setbacks.

5. **Be Prepared to Take Action:** Lastly, we need to be prepared to take action when the opportunity we've always hoped for presents itself. This means being confident, taking risks, and having a plan in place to make the most of the opportunity. We should be prepared to work hard and seize the moment when it arises.

Staying ready for opportunities requires commitment, dedication, and a positive mindset. By defining our goals, continuing to learn and grow, building relationships, staying positive, and being prepared to take action, we can stay ready for the opportunities we've always hoped for.

Preparing for opportunities is a continuous process that requires consistent effort and a proactive approach. By following the steps outlined, we can increase our chances of being prepared for the opportunities that come our way.

Defining our goals and being prepared involves identifying what we want to achieve and outlining the steps we need to take to achieve it. This means setting realistic and achievable goals, creating a plan of action, and being prepared to adapt to changing circumstances.

Continuing to learn and grow is crucial in staying ready for opportunities. This involves seeking out new knowledge, acquiring new skills, and staying up-to-date with the latest trends and developments in our field. This can help us stay competitive and better prepared to seize opportunities as they arise.

Building relationships and networking can also be essential in staying ready for opportunities. By connecting with like-minded people, attending industry events, and joining professional associations, we can increase our visibility and expand our network, making it more likely that we will be in the right place at the right time.

If you are a man seeking to expand his family, it is crucial to prepare daily for your journey as the leader of your growing family. As a wife within the Divine Family Unit arrangement, it is crucial to make sure that you prepare for your husband's journey in expanding the family as well. Utilizing these best practices and being intentional with the direction you have agreed to will assist in normalizing your decision, and keep you prepared for the day your family does expand.

As the husband of your family, you don't want to miss a great opportunity with a potential wife because you daydreamed about the possibilities of leading an expanded family, but never put action steps into motion that would help you reach your goal and vision.

If you are the wife or wives in an expanded family, you want to maintain your ability to prepare by recognizing that your roles and position in the family do not have to be threatened or diminished in any way.

When you prepare yourself as a foundational wife for the possibility of an incoming wife, you will have done everything in your power to ensure that raw emotion and jealousy about your husband's choices and decisions will be at a minimum. You will continue to be a helpmate to your husband, and help to alleviate the anxiousness surrounding him bringing a new wife into the Divine Family dynamic.

Staying positive and focused is also important in staying ready for opportunities. By maintaining a positive mindset and visualizing our goals, we can stay motivated and persistent, even in the face of challenges and setbacks. This can help us stay on track and keep working towards our goals.

Finally, being prepared to take action means being confident, taking risks, and having a plan in place to make the most of the opportunity. This involves being prepared to work hard and make sacrifices, but also being open to new experiences and opportunities.

Overall, staying ready for opportunities requires a combination of dedication, hard work, and a positive attitude. By following these steps, and keeping parables like the one HaMashiach spoke close to heart, we can increase our chances of being prepared for the opportunities we've always hoped for.

10

THE STORY OF MOSES AND HIS TWO WIVES

Wait A Minute...Moses Had Two Wives?

The story of Moses and his two wives is a lesser-known aspect of the life of Moses, one of the most prominent figures in the Bible and Quran. According to the biblical account, Moses had two wives, Zipporah and an Ethiopian woman named in some translations as Cushite or Midianite.

The story of Moses and his first wife, Zipporah, is well-known. She was the daughter of Jethro, a Midianite priest, whom Moses met while he was fleeing from Egypt. After helping Moses, Jethro gave his daughter Zipporah to him in marriage.

However, the story of Moses' second wife is less commonly known. The woman is referred to in the Bible as a Cushite or Midianite woman, but her name is not mentioned. Some scholars believe that she may have been from Ethiopia or a neighboring region. According to the Bible, Aaron and

Miriam, Moses' siblings, were critical of Moses' marriage to this woman, citing her ethnic background as the reason for their disapproval.

In the book of Numbers, chapter 12, it is recorded that Aaron and Miriam spoke against Moses because of his Cushite wife. They said, "Has the Lord indeed spoken only through Moses? Has he not spoken through us also?" This criticism of Moses' leadership prompted God to intervene and rebuke Aaron and Miriam for their jealousy and lack of respect for Moses.

It is unclear what happened to Moses' second wife, but some scholars believe that she may have died before the events recorded in the Book of Numbers. Others suggest that she may have been divorced or separated from Moses at some point.

The story of Moses and his two wives is a reminder that even the most revered figures in Israelite history had personal struggles and relationships that were not always perfect. Moses' marriages to two women of different ethnic backgrounds demonstrate that diversity has always been a part of Israelite, as well as human history and that our differences should be celebrated rather than used as a source of division.

So Who Exactly Is Moses?

Moses is one of the most significant figures in the Bible and is considered a central figure in Israelite History, Christianity, and Islam. He is credited with leading the Israelites out of slavery in Egypt and receiving the Ten Commandments from God on Mount Sinai.

According to the biblical account, Moses was born to Hebrew parents during a time when the Pharaoh of Egypt had ordered the death of all male Hebrew babies. To save his life, Moses' mother placed him in a basket and set him afloat on the Nile River. The basket was found by the Pharaoh's daughter, who raised Moses as her own.

As Moses grew up, he became aware of his Hebrew heritage and witnessed the harsh treatment of his people by the Egyptians. One day, he killed an Egyptian who was mistreating a Hebrew slave, and he had to flee Egypt to avoid being punished.

While in exile in the land of Midian, Moses encountered God in the form of a burning bush. God told Moses to return to Egypt and lead the Israelites out of slavery. Moses initially hesitated, but God provided him with miraculous signs to demonstrate his power and convince him to carry out his mission.

Moses returned to Egypt and, with the help of his brother Aaron, confronted the Pharaoh, demanding that he release the Israelites. The Pharaoh refused, and God sent a series of ten plagues upon Egypt to demonstrate his power and force the Pharaoh to release the Israelites.

After the tenth plague, in which the firstborn sons of Egypt were killed, the Pharaoh finally relented, and Moses led the Israelites out of Egypt. God parted the Red Sea so that the Israelites could cross on dry land, and then closed the waters back over the pursuing Egyptian army.

Moses then led the Israelites through the wilderness for 40 years, during which time he received the Ten Commandments from God on Mount Sinai. He also received other laws and commandments, which are recorded in the books of Exodus, Leviticus, Numbers, and Deuteronomy.

Despite his great leadership and devotion to God, Moses was not without flaws. He struggled with anger and impatience at times and was prevented by God from entering the promised land because of a mistake he made in striking a rock to bring forth water instead of speaking to it as God commanded.

Moses is remembered as a great prophet and leader who delivered the Israelites from slavery and established the foundation for their religious and cultural traditions. His story continues to inspire and inform the beliefs and practices of millions of people around the world today.

The First Women In Moses' Life

Shiprah and Jochebed are two important women mentioned in the biblical story of Moses. However, did you know that Jochebed, Moses' mother, was also Shiprah, one of two Hebrew midwives who helped deliver Moses and save his life?

According to the biblical account in Exodus chapter 1, the Pharaoh of Egypt became afraid of the growing population of Hebrews and ordered that all male Hebrew babies be killed at birth. However, Jochebed gave birth to Moses and was determined to save his life. She placed him in a basket and set him afloat on the Nile River, hoping that someone would find him and take him in.

Shiprah and the other midwife, Puah, who was Moses' older sister, Miriam, were instructed by the Pharaoh to carry out his orders and kill any male Hebrew babies they delivered. However, they disobeyed this command and allowed the male babies to live. When the Pharaoh demanded an explanation, they claimed that the Hebrew women were giving birth before they could arrive and that they were powerless to prevent it.

Many Rabbinic traditions identify Shiprah with Jochebed, Moses' mother. The name Shiprah is said to mean "beautiful" or "adorned" in Hebrew, and it is believed that she was given this name because of her skill as a midwife in cleansing and caring for newborns.

Some Rabbinic traditions also suggest that Shiprah's name is derived from the Hebrew word "she-paru," which means "they multiplied." This is based on the belief that the Israelites continued to multiply and prosper when Shiprah was helping to deliver their babies. It is said that she was blessed by God with fertility and that she gave birth to many children. She gave birth to the future leaders of the children of Israel. This was part of her reward for being obedient to The Highest instead of listening to Pharaoh's orders to kill any male Israelite babies they delivered.

Regardless of the etymology of her name, Shiprah's role in the story of Moses is an important one. Along with Puah, she defied the Pharaoh's orders and risked her life to save the lives of innocent babies. Her compassion and bravery are an inspiration to all who read her story.

Moses was eventually found by the Pharaoh's daughter, who raised him as her own. Jochebed was eventually summoned to nurse him and was paid for her services. This allowed her to remain close to her son and continue to care for him.

The story of Shiprah and Puah, who were also Moses' mother and elder sister, demonstrates the courage and faith of these midwives in the face of great danger.

They defied the orders of a powerful ruler and risked their own lives to save the lives of innocent babies. Their actions were an act of resistance against the oppressive regime of the Pharaoh, and they helped to preserve the future of the Hebrew people.

Jochebed's role as Moses' mother is also significant. Her willingness to risk everything to save her son's life is a testament to the strength and love of a mother's bond. She not only gave birth to Moses but also had the wisdom and courage to entrust him to the care of others who could help him survive.

Together, the stories of Shiprah, and Puah, also known as Jochebed and Miriam, illustrate the importance of standing up for what is right, even in the face of great danger, and the power of a mother's love to overcome adversity. Their actions helped to shape the destiny of Moses and the Israelites and continue to inspire people today.

Who Was Zipporah?

Zipporah was the wife of Moses, the great prophet and leader of the Israelites. According to the biblical account in Exodus chapter 2, Moses fled from Egypt to the land of Midian after he killed an Egyptian who was beating a Hebrew slave. In Midian, Moses met Zipporah, the daughter of a priest named Jethro (also known as Reuel), and he married her.

Zipporah played an important role in Moses' life, especially during his time in Midian. She was a faithful and supportive wife, and she stood by Moses through many challenges and difficulties. When Moses was called by God to return to Egypt and lead the Israelites out of slavery, Zipporah and their two sons joined him on the journey.

There is also a famous story in Exodus chapter 4 about Zipporah saving Moses' life. As Moses was traveling back to Egypt, God appeared to him and threatened to kill him because he had not circumcised his son. Zipporah quickly circumcised their son and touched Moses' feet with the foreskin, thus satisfying God and preventing Moses' death.

In addition to this, Zipporah is also mentioned in Exodus chapter 18, where

Jethro comes to visit Moses and the Israelites in the desert. Jethro advises Moses to appoint judges to help him with the task of governing the people, and he also offers a sacrifice to God. Zipporah and their two sons are present during this visit, but they are not mentioned again in the biblical account after this.

Overall, Zipporah was a loyal and supportive wife to Moses, and her quick thinking and action saved his life on one occasion. Her role in Moses' life may not be as prominent as that of other biblical figures, but her presence is a reminder of the importance of having a supportive and faithful partner in one's life.

Moses' Second Wife Was An Ethiopian Woman

In the biblical account found in Numbers 12:1, Moses' second wife is described as "a Cushite woman." Cushite refers to a person from the region of Cush, which is often identified as modern-day Ethiopia.

The woman's name is not given in the biblical text, but some scholars believe that she may have been Zipporah, Moses' first wife, who was also known as a Midianite. However, others argue that she was a different woman altogether, possibly someone that Moses married during his time as a leader of the Israelites.

The story of Moses' second wife is not well-developed in the biblical account, but it is mentioned in the context of a dispute between Moses' siblings, Aaron and Miriam, and Moses himself. According to the story, Aaron and Miriam criticized Moses for marrying a Cushite woman, and they claimed that God spoke to them just as he did to Moses.

God became angry at Aaron and Miriam for their arrogance and punished Miriam with leprosy.

The identity and background of Moses' second wife remain a topic of debate and speculation among scholars and religious commentators. However, the story highlights the challenges and conflicts that can arise within families and communities, even among people who are called to serve God.

How To Be A Supportive Wife Of A Husband Who Is A Leader

Moses will forever be known as one of the greatest leaders of people to have ever existed. He was a devoted man, who had a calling over his life that could not be denied. His wives were super supportive of him, even though their lives together were difficult to endure at times.

Many Israelite men seek to emulate Moses at one point in their lives. We have a deep desire to be great men, and to be used by The Most High to do something of service for Him. When we have a wife, or wives who support the calling on our life, we can do absolutely anything that The Most High has called us to do, no matter the level of difficulty involved with the mission.

Being a supportive wife to a husband who is a leader can be a challenging but rewarding role. Here are some best practices on how to be a supportive wife of a husband who is a leader:

1. **Show respect:** Respect your husband's position as a leader, even if you disagree with some of his decisions. Show respect by listening

attentively to his ideas and suggestions, and by offering constructive feedback when necessary.

2. **Be a sounding board:** Leaders often face difficult decisions and challenges, and they need someone to talk to and bounce ideas off of. Be a supportive wife by being a listening ear and providing feedback and guidance when needed.

3. **Encourage and motivate:** Leaders need encouragement and motivation to keep going, especially during tough times. Be a supportive wife by offering words of encouragement and motivation when your husband is feeling down or discouraged. Your husband may face challenges and obstacles in pursuing his calling from God. As his wife, it's important to be his biggest supporter and cheerleader. Encourage him to pursue his calling with passion and commitment, and remind him of his strengths and abilities.

4. **Help with practical tasks:** Being a leader often requires a lot of work, and your husband may not have the time or energy to take care of everything. Be a supportive wife by helping with practical tasks such as running errands, cooking meals, or taking care of the children.

5. **Be flexible:** Leaders often have unpredictable schedules and may need to attend meetings or events at short notice. Be a supportive wife by being flexible and accommodating your husband's schedule as much as possible. Pursuing a calling from God can also be a demanding journey. So remember to be flexible and understanding of your husband's schedule, as he may need to attend meetings, and events, or travel frequently.

6. **Stay positive:** Being a supportive wife means staying optimistic even during challenging times. Avoid complaining or criticizing your husband in public or around others, and try to maintain a positive attitude. Believe in your husband's calling and his ability to make a difference, and continue to support him through the ups and downs of his journey.

7. **Take care of yourself:** Finally, remember to take care of yourself as well. Being a supportive wife can be demanding, and it's important

to take time for yourself to recharge and refresh so that you can be at your best for your husband and family. Being a supportive wife can also be emotionally and physically challenging, so it's important to make sure to prioritize self-care because supporting your husband while he walks in his calling is super important.

8. **Pray with and for him:** Prayer is a powerful tool that can help your husband stay connected to his faith and his calling. Pray with your husband regularly, and also pray for him when he's facing challenges or needs guidance.

9. **Help him discern God's will:** Your husband may struggle at times to discern God's will for his life and his calling. Be a supportive wife by helping him think through decisions and offering guidance when needed. Encourage him to seek counsel from trusted mentors or religious leaders as well.

10. **Be a good listener:** Your husband may need someone to talk to about his struggles, his successes, and his doubts. Be a good listener, and offer support and encouragement when needed.

Moses was a great leader who faced many challenges and obstacles in his journey. From leading the Israelites out of slavery in Egypt to receiving the Ten Commandments on Mount Sinai, Moses' mission from God was a challenging one.

Despite the difficulties he faced, Moses persevered and did his best to guide the Israelites and his family. He showed great strength, courage, and faith in the face of adversity, and his leadership inspired many.

Moses' story is a reminder that being a leader is not an easy task and that it requires a lot of hard work, dedication, and sacrifice. But with the help of God, anything is possible, and even the most daunting challenges can be overcome.

So, as you set out to grow your Divine Family Unit, please remember to stay motivated like Moses and keep in mind that nothing worth having is going to be easy to obtain. Our families are going to require a different form of maturity from us as we cultivate them. Let's keep this in mind as we make decisions that will greatly affect everyone involved.

This is why we pray daily that the decisions we choose are in Divine alignment with The Most High's Will for us.

11

HOW TO MAINTAIN PEACE AND STRUCTURE AT HOME WHEN YOU HAVE MULTIPLE WIVES

Do Know This: Marriage Ain't Easy!

R egardless of how many wives you have, marriage is not always easy, and couples face a wide range of challenges daily. However, with the right mindset and approach, any challenge can be overcome.

Understanding is a critical component of a successful marriage. Couples must make an effort to understand each other's perspectives, feelings, and needs. When we understand our partners, we are more likely to empathize with them, communicate effectively, and avoid unnecessary conflicts.

Patience is another essential element of a successful marriage. Couples need to be patient with each other, especially when facing difficult situations or when going through a tough time. Patience allows us to take a step back, evaluate the situation, and find constructive solutions.

In addition to understanding and patience, successful marriages also require other key elements such as love, respect, trust, and communication. These elements are essential to building a strong and healthy relationship.

It is also important for couples to have realistic expectations of each other and their marriage. Marriage is not always going to be perfect, and there will be challenges along the way. But with understanding, patience, and a willingness to work through issues together, couples can overcome any challenge and build a stronger relationship.

Overcoming Challenges Together

Married couples can overcome any challenge when they approach their problems with understanding and patience. By focusing on the key elements of a successful marriage and having realistic expectations, couples can build a strong and healthy relationship that lasts a lifetime.

Maintaining peace and structure at home is crucial in any household, regardless of the number of wives or family members. However, being married to multiple wives presents unique challenges that require specific strategies to ensure harmony and happiness in the home. Here are some tips for maintaining peace and structure at home when you are married to multiple wives:

1. **Communication:** Communication is essential in any relationship, and it becomes even more crucial when dealing with multiple wives. Ensure that you maintain open and honest communication with all your wives. Encourage them to speak their minds and express their opinions, and be willing to listen to their concerns.

2. **Fairness:** It's crucial to be fair to all your wives. Treat them equally and avoid showing favoritism. This can cause resentment and division among your wives, leading to conflict and tension in the home.

3. **Respect:** Respect is a fundamental value in any relationship, and it's especially important when you are married to multiple wives. Ensure that you show respect to each of your wives and their individual beliefs and values. Avoid belittling or demeaning them, as this can cause hurt and damage to the relationship.

4. **Boundaries:** Establish clear boundaries in your relationships with each of your wives. Respect their individual spaces and privacy, and avoid interfering in their alone time while they are focused on introspection and reflection. This can help prevent conflict and maintain a peaceful and harmonious home.

5. **Time management:** Managing your time effectively is crucial when you are married to multiple wives. Ensure that you spend quality time with each of your wives, and avoid neglecting one wife over the others. This can help build strong relationships with each of your wives and maintain a peaceful home.

6. **Conflict resolution:** Conflict is inevitable in any relationship, and it's essential to know how to handle conflicts when they arise. Encourage your wives to communicate their issues openly and honestly, and work together to find a resolution that works for everyone.

7. **Support:** Finally, ensure that you support each of your wives emotionally and physically. Be there for them when they need you and offer them a safe and supportive environment to thrive in.

Cultivating shalom and structure at home when you are married to multiple wives requires open communication, fairness, respect, boundaries, time management, compromise, conflict resolution, and support. By implementing these strategies, you can build strong relationships with each of your wives and maintain a peaceful, structured, and harmonious home.

Marriage is a partnership that requires both parties to actively listen to each other and work together to overcome any challenges that arise. Effective communication and compromise are essential to maintaining a healthy and successful marriage.

In a marriage, it's important to recognize that each person has their strengths, weaknesses, and perspectives. By listening to each other's concerns, couples can gain a better understanding of each other and work together to find solutions that work for both parties. Additionally, by acknowledging and appreciating each other's strengths, couples can work together to leverage those strengths to overcome challenges.

Successful marriages are also characterized by a commitment to working towards shared goals. This means that couples need to be willing to put in the effort and time to achieve the outcomes they desire, whether that's building a strong financial foundation, raising a family, or pursuing personal and professional goals.

Overall, a successful marriage requires both partners to be committed to working together, communicating effectively, and being willing to put in the effort to overcome challenges and achieve their shared goals.

12

HOW TO BUILD A STABLE STRUCTURE FOR YOUR HOUSEHOLD

Your Household Won't Build Itself

As you continue to grow and cultivate your family, it's important to gain some insights about building a stable structure for your household.

Creating a stable household structure involves creating a supportive environment for everyone in the family to thrive. This includes establishing clear communication, setting boundaries, and providing emotional and physical support.

Clear communication involves being honest and open with each other, actively listening to one another, and respectfully expressing feelings. It's also important to establish boundaries to respect each other's privacy and personal space.

Providing emotional and physical support involves being there for each other during challenging times, offering help when needed, and creating a nurturing environment that promotes well-being. This can include engaging in family activities, providing nutritious meals, and creating a safe and comfortable living space.

In addition to creating a stable household structure, it's also important to have financial stability. This includes budgeting, saving money, and planning for the future to ensure that the family's basic needs are met and that there is a secure financial future.

Overall, building a stable household structure involves creating a supportive and nurturing environment that promotes emotional, physical, and financial well-being for everyone in the family.

Taking Steps In The Right Direction

There are several steps you can take to build a stable structure for your household and make plans for your family's future:

1. **Establish clear communication:** Communication is the foundation of a stable household structure. It's important to have open and honest communication with your family members, to listen actively to their concerns, and to express your feelings respectfully. This helps to build trust and promotes healthy relationships within the family.
2. **Set boundaries:** Setting boundaries is important to respect each other's privacy and personal space. This can include establishing rules around personal belongings, screen time, and socializing. By setting

clear boundaries, everyone in the household knows what is expected of them and can avoid conflicts that may arise from misunderstandings.

3. **Create a nurturing environment:** Creating a nurturing environment involves providing emotional and physical support to your family members. This can include engaging in family activities, providing nutritious meals, and creating a safe and comfortable living space. By creating a nurturing environment, you can help your family members feel valued, supported, and loved.

4. **Plan for the future:** It's important to plan for the future to ensure that your family's basic needs are met and that there is a secure financial future. This can involve creating a budget, saving money, and investing in long-term goals such as retirement or education. By planning for the future, you can help your family members feel more secure and confident about their prospects.

5. **Seek help when needed:** If you're struggling to build a stable household structure or make plans for your family's future, it's important to seek help when needed. This may involve talking to a trusted friend or family member, seeking advice from a professional, or joining a support group. Remember, you don't have to do everything on your own, and there are resources available to help you build a stable and successful household structure.

There are many factors to consider when making decisions that can impact your family's well-being, including financial, emotional, and social considerations.

Making the right decisions for your family is not always easy, and requires careful thought and consideration. It's important to weigh the potential risks and benefits of any decision and to consider how it may impact each family member individually as well as the family as a whole. It can be helpful to seek input and advice from trusted friends or family members and to do your research to ensure you have all the information you need to make an informed decision.

It's also important to recognize that there may be times when you make a decision that doesn't turn out as you had hoped. In these situations, it's important to take responsibility for your actions, learn from your mistakes, and make adjustments as needed.

Remember, making the right decisions for your family is an ongoing process that requires flexibility, patience, and a willingness to adapt as circumstances change. With time and practice, you can develop the skills and confidence you need to make decisions that are in the best interests of your family.

13

HOW TO BE THE MAN IN YOUR HOUSEHOLD

Love, Vision, And Support

Being a loving, visionary, and supportive husband is essential for a healthy and functional household dynamic. These qualities help create a strong bond between partners, set long-term goals, and work together as a team to overcome challenges. A husband who embodies these qualities can create a loving and supportive environment for his family, which can lead to a happy and fulfilling household dynamic.

While it is true that all members of a household depend on each other to meet their needs and requirements for growth, it is important to note that this is not solely the responsibility of the husband or father. In a healthy and functional household dynamic, all members share the responsibility of meeting each other's needs and contributing to the growth and well-being of the family.

That being said, the role of a husband and father in a household is certainly multifaceted and complex. The husband needs to be attentive to the needs of each member of the family and work collaboratively with his partner to create a nurturing and supportive environment for everyone.

As a loving husband and father, it is important to prioritize the needs and well-being of each family member. This means taking the time to listen and understand their concerns, being emotionally available and supportive, and taking an active role in household duties and child-rearing. It also means setting long-term goals for the family and working together as a team to achieve them.

In addition, a visionary husband and father is someone who can see beyond the immediate needs and challenges of the family and plan for the future. This includes setting financial goals, planning for education and career opportunities, and creating a stable and secure future for the family.

Ultimately, the role of a husband and father in a household is to be a supportive and loving partner and parent, who can lead and inspire their family to grow and thrive. It is a collaborative effort where everyone's contributions and needs are valued and respected.

The Role Of A Husband

While it is true that some women may appreciate a man who can lead and take charge in certain situations, it is important to note that every person has unique preferences and priorities when it comes to relationships. It is also important to recognize that the idea of a man "leading" a woman in modern times can sometimes imply a power dynamic that is not conducive to healthy and equal relationships.

Achieving this dynamic will take some patience and effort on your part as the man and husband. It's important to keep modern societal perspectives out of your marriage, or marriages, as much as possible.

The role of a husband in a household is multifaceted and complex. Being a loving, visionary, and supportive husband is crucial for a healthy and functional household dynamic. Let's take a closer look at each of these qualities:

1. **Loving:** Love is the foundation of any healthy relationship. A loving husband is affectionate, empathetic, and kind towards his partner. He takes the time to listen and understand their needs and wants and is always there to offer emotional support. A husband who is loving towards his partner creates a strong bond between them, which is essential for a happy household.

2. **Visionary:** A visionary husband is someone who is forward-thinking and has a clear idea of the future they want to build for their family. He sets long-term goals and works towards them with dedication and passion. He is open to new ideas and perspectives and collaborates with his partner to make decisions that benefit the family as a whole. A visionary husband is an inspiration for his family and encourages them to strive for excellence.

3. **Supportive:** A supportive husband is someone who is always there for his partner and family. He offers emotional and practical support whenever needed, and is willing to make sacrifices to ensure the well-being of his loved ones. A supportive husband is an equal partner in household duties and takes an active role in raising children. He is willing to work together with his partner to overcome challenges and build a strong, resilient family.

In a healthy and functional relationship, all consenting adults should be able to communicate openly and honestly with each other and should be willing to listen to each other's concerns and opinions. This means that a man who can listen to his wife's concerns and offer support and guidance like a counselor can be incredibly valuable in a relationship.

Effective communication is key in any relationship, and being able to listen and empathize with your wife's concerns is essential for building trust and emotional intimacy. A man who can offer emotional support and guidance to his partner can create a strong and nurturing relationship dynamic, where both partners feel valued and respected.

In addition, it is important to recognize that a man who can listen to his wife's concerns and prioritize her needs is not necessarily a "counselor", but rather a loving and supportive partner. Both partners should be willing to support and uplift each other and work together as a team to navigate the challenges and joys of life.

Ultimately, every relationship is unique, and there is no one-size-fits-all approach to building a healthy and fulfilling partnership. Both spouses need to communicate openly and honestly with each other and prioritize each other's needs and well-being in all aspects of the relationship.

14

MAKING THE NECESSARY ADJUSTMENTS WHEN ADDING A WIFE TO YOUR FAMILY

Making adjustments is crucial when you have goals and aspirations that you want to achieve in life. As you progress towards your goals, you may encounter unexpected challenges or obstacles, and it is essential to be able to adjust your plans accordingly to stay on track.

Furthermore, as you gain new experiences and learn more about yourself and your environment, your priorities and aspirations may shift. Thus, you need to be open to making adjustments to your plans to ensure that they align with your current goals and aspirations.

Being flexible and adaptable in your approach to achieving your goals is essential to ensure that you can overcome obstacles, stay on track, and make progress toward your completing your objectives.

Flexibility and adaptability are crucial traits to have when pursuing your goals because they allow you to adjust your approach based on changing circumstances and unexpected obstacles. By being flexible and adaptable, you can overcome challenges, stay focused on your goals, and make progress toward achieving your aspirations.

Being rigid and inflexible can lead to frustration and disappointment, as unexpected circumstances can easily derail your plans. However, by embracing flexibility and adaptability, you can view unexpected obstacles as opportunities to learn and grow, which can help you stay motivated and engaged in the pursuit of your goals.

In regards to the expanded family, please expect to be shunned by those who you thought would be the most supportive of your decision to establish your Divine Family Unit. Oftentimes, those closest to us will not understand, or seek to understand for that matter, why your goal to establish your Divine Family Unit is important to you; don't let the negative attitudes and mindsets of any naysayers deter you from your pursuit to grow your family.

Once you have decided on a pursuit or goal, standing your ground is crucial, especially when dealing with unsupportive family members. It can be challenging to pursue your goals when you feel like those closest to you don't understand or support your choices.

However, it's important to remember that your goals and aspirations are yours alone, and you are entitled to pursue them regardless of others' opinions.

Your life path journey is your own, and you must make your own choices and follow your dreams. Stay true to yourself, and don't let anyone else's doubts or opinions hold you back from achieving your goals.

Dealing with friends and family members who do not understand your vision or goals can be challenging, but there are ways to handle the situation. Here are a few strategies to help you stand your ground and stay true to your goals:

1. **Communicate Clearly:** Make sure that you communicate your goals and aspirations clearly to your family members. Explain why you have chosen this path and how it aligns with your values and interests. Listen to their concerns and try to address them respectfully and constructively.

2. **Stay Confident:** Be confident in yourself and your vision. Believe in yourself and your ability to achieve your goals, even if others don't understand or support your choices.

3. **Seek Support Outside Your Family:** Look for support outside your family, such as true friends, mentors, or like-minded individuals who share your vision and can provide encouragement and guidance. If your family members are not supportive, it's essential to seek support from other sources, such as friends, mentors, or like-minded individuals who share your vision and can provide encouragement and guidance.

4. **Set Boundaries:** It's important to set boundaries with family members who do not support your goals. Respectfully let them know that you appreciate their concern but that you have made your decision and need their support.

5. **Focus on the Positive:** Try to focus on the positive aspects of your relationship with your family members and find common ground where you can connect. Celebrate your successes with them, and be open to sharing your journey with them over time.

6. **Be Clear About Your Goals:** Make sure that you have a clear understanding of your goals and why you want to pursue them. This will help you communicate your intentions more effectively to your family members and give you a stronger sense of conviction.

7. **Stay Focused:** Stay focused on your goals and avoid getting side-tracked by the opinions or doubts of others. It's important to stay motivated and committed to your pursuit, even when faced with

challenges or setbacks.

8. **Practice Self-Care:** Pursuing your goals can be stressful, especially when dealing with unsupportive family members. It's important to take care of yourself and practice self-care to stay resilient and maintain your mental and emotional well-being.

9. **Celebrate Your Successes:** Celebrate your successes, no matter how small, and acknowledge the progress you've made towards your goals. This will help you stay motivated and reinforce your commitment to your pursuit.

Remember, the path to achieving your goals is not always a straight line, and it may require detours, adjustments, and changes along the way. The ability to be flexible and adaptable in your approach can make all the difference in achieving your aspirations. Standing your ground and pursuing your goals takes courage, resilience, and conviction.

Don't be afraid to stay true to yourself and follow your dreams, even in the face of adversity.

What is Romanticism, Like For Real?

As a Hebrew Israelite, still, in the place of your captivity, it is crucial to understand the system that you have been placed in. It is just as important to recognize the extremes in cultural differences that cause many of us to not see the bigger picture in regards to the control and domination of the Roman Empire still in power and worldwide governance today.

If you have decided to grow and expand your family, it is paramount that you learn about this system, as well as the system of your ancestral estate, and how these two systems differ from one another. Once you arm yourself with a clearer perspective on what Western Influence is, you will be more adept at guiding your Divine Family Unit in a righteous and upstanding way.

Romanticism is an artistic and literary movement that originated in Europe towards the end of the 18th century and lasted until the mid-19th century. It is characterized by an emphasis on emotion, imagination, individualism, and nature.

Romanticism was a reaction against the Enlightenment, which emphasized reason, logic, and scientific rationality, and against the Industrial Revolution, which brought about unprecedented changes in society, technology, and the economy. Romantics sought to express their feelings and experiences in a way that reflected their subjective reality, rather than conforming to objective standards of rationality and order.

Romantic literature often featured themes of love, nature, and the supernatural, and emphasized the role of the individual in shaping their destiny. Poets like William Wordsworth, Samuel Taylor Coleridge, and John Keats celebrated the beauty of nature and explored the power of the imagination. Novelists like Jane Austen and the Bronte sisters explored the emotional and psychological experiences of women in society.

In art, Romanticism emphasized emotion, drama, and intense color, and often featured dramatic landscapes and scenes from history or mythology. Artists like Eugène Delacroix and Francisco Goya were known for their bold and expressive brushstrokes, while J.M.W. Turner was celebrated for his atmospheric landscapes.

Overall, Romanticism represented a new way of thinking about art, literature, and culture, emphasizing the power of emotion, the importance of individual experience, and the beauty of nature. Its influence can still be seen in many forms of art and literature today.

Romanticism has also had its influence on the sphere of how people all over the world view themselves when it comes to the emotions of love and passion. People of different nations and cultures all over the earth have in one way or another felt the impact of Romanticism, and it hasn't always been the fairytale ending that they expected it to be.

One important aspect that must be grasped is that the Roman way of thinking is the total and polar opposite of the Hebraic way of thinking. The two frames of thought are constantly at war whether we've recognized it or not. This war has had lasting effects spanning multiple generations, even up to the present day.

The subject of expanded family is a threat to Romanticism, while the idea of monogamy has always served as the catalyst for an expanded family within the Hebraic frame of thought. In other words: monogamy is not a threat to the Hebraic or Roman way of life, but polygyny, a Hebraic cultural way of living, is a threat to the Roman way of living.

The threat that the Hebraic expanded family presents to the Roman mindset has always been rooted in the need for the Roman Empire to take control of and domineer over all other nations on earth, while at the same time forcing its viewpoints on those who are placed under their dominion.

When we take the influence of Rome, and apply it to a modernized viewpoint, we arrive at what is commonly referred to as the Western Influence. Western influence refers to the impact that the cultures and values of Western Europe and North America have had on the rest of the world. This influence has been particularly strong since the 19th century when Western powers began to expand their territories and establish colonies in other parts of the world.

The roots of Western influence can be traced back to the ancient Greeks, who made significant contributions to philosophy, literature, art, and science. Their ideas and achievements were later preserved and transmitted by the Romans, who also made important contributions to Western culture.

During the Middle Ages, Western Europe experienced a period of cultural and intellectual growth known as the Renaissance, which saw a renewed interest in classical Greek and Roman culture. This led to the development of humanism, a philosophy that emphasized the value of human experience and individualism.

In the 17th and 18th centuries, the Enlightenment saw the rise of new ideas about reason, science, and individual rights. These ideas were reflected in the political revolutions that took place in Europe and North America during this period, including the American Revolution and the French Revolution.

In the 19th century, Western powers began to expand their territories and establish colonies in other parts of the world, spreading their culture and values to other regions. This process of colonization and cultural exchange continued throughout the 20th century, with the United States emerging as a dominant cultural and economic power.

Today, Western influence can be seen in many aspects of global culture, including fashion, music, film, literature, and technology. However, it has also been criticized for its role in promoting cultural homogenization and undermining local traditions and identities.

Understanding the effects of Western influence on the rest of the world is a complex and multifaceted task, as the impact of Western culture and values has been felt in different ways in different regions and at different times. However, several key factors can help us to understand this impact:

1. **Historical context:** Understanding the historical context in which

Western influence developed is crucial to understanding its effects on the rest of the world. This includes understanding the history of colonialism, imperialism, and globalization, as well as the political, economic, and cultural dynamics that have shaped the relationship between the West and the rest of the world.

2. **Cultural exchange:** Western influence has been driven by a process of cultural exchange, in which Western ideas, values, and practices have been adopted and adapted by people in other parts of the world. Understanding how this exchange has taken place, and how it has been received and interpreted in different cultural contexts, is key to understanding its effects.

3. **Power dynamics:** Western influence has often been associated with power and domination, as Western powers have sought to impose their values and institutions on other parts of the world. Understanding the power dynamics involved in this process is important for understanding its effects on different societies and cultures.

4. **Resistance and adaptation:** Despite the power dynamics involved in Western influence, people in other parts of the world have also resisted and adapted to Western culture and values in various ways. Understanding how people have adapted, challenged, and transformed Western influence is important for understanding its long-term effects.

Overall, understanding the effects of Western influence on the rest of the world requires a nuanced and context-specific approach, which takes into account historical, cultural, political, and economic factors, as well as the agency of individuals and groups in shaping the impact of Western culture and values.

What Does It Mean To Have A Hebraic Mindset?

Hebraic Israelite thought refers to the intellectual and cultural traditions of the Israelite people, which are based on the Hebrew Bible, also known as the Old Testament, or more traditionally, the Tanakh. These traditions emphasize a holistic approach to understanding the world that integrates spiritual, ethical, and practical concerns.

One of the key features of Hebraic Israelite thought is its emphasis on the importance of action and practice, rather than just belief or abstract ideas. This is reflected in Israelite ethical and religious practices, such as observing the Sabbath, following dietary laws, and engaging in acts of charity and social justice.

Hebraic Israelite thought is also characterized by a strong sense of community and the importance of collective responsibility. This is reflected in Israelite and Ishmaelite traditions such as the emphasis on family, the obligation to care for the poor and needy, and the importance of maintaining social justice.

Another key aspect of Hebraic Israelite thought is its emphasis on the study and interpretation of sacred texts. This tradition places a high value on the study of the Torah and other Israelite-based texts and has given rise to a rich tradition of Israelite scholarship and interpretation.

Hebraic Israelite thought has had a significant impact on world history and culture, particularly through its influence on the Abrahamic religions (Judaism, Christianity, and Islam). Many of the core beliefs and practices of these religions are based on Hebraic Israelite traditions, and the Bible has had a profound impact on world literature and culture.

Overall, Hebraic Israelite thought emphasizes the importance of living a life that is both spiritually fulfilling and socially responsible and has had a profound impact on the history, culture, and values of the Israelite people and the world as a whole.

Understanding the impact of Israelite thought and influence on the rest of the world requires an examination of several key factors, including historical context, cultural exchange, power dynamics, and adaptation.

1. **Historical context:** Understanding the historical context in which Israelite thought developed is crucial to understanding its impact on the rest of the world. This includes understanding the history of the Israelites, the development of the Hebrew Bible, and the impact of Hebraic thought on world history.
2. **Cultural exchange:** Israelite thought has been disseminated through cultural exchange, in which Israelite ideas, values, and practices have been adopted and adapted by people in other parts of the world. Understanding how this exchange has taken place, and how it has been received and interpreted in different cultural contexts, is key to understanding its effects.
3. **Power dynamics:** Israelite thought has often been associated with power and domination, as Israelite communities have sought to maintain their cultural and religious identity in the face of persecution and oppression. Understanding the power dynamics involved in this process is important for understanding its impact on different societies and cultures.
4. **Resistance and adaptation:** Despite the power dynamics involved in Israelite thought, people in other parts of the world have also resisted and adapted Israelite culture and values in various ways. Understanding how people have adapted, challenged, and transformed Israelite thought is important for understanding its long-term impact.
5. **Literature:** The Bible, which is the foundation of Hebraic thought, has had a significant impact on world literature. Many of the stories,

themes, and characters from the Hebrew Bible have been adapted and reinterpreted in works of literature from around the world.

6. **Ethics:** The ethical principles of Hebraic thought have had a profound impact on Western ethical and moral traditions. The idea of treating others with compassion and justice, as well as the concept of the sanctity of life, are deeply rooted in Israelite thought.

7. **Religion:** Hebraic thought has had a profound impact on the development of the Abrahamic religions, including Judaism, Christianity, and Islam. Many of the core beliefs and practices of these religions are based on Hebraic traditions.

8. **Philosophy:** Hebraic thought has also influenced the development of Western philosophy, particularly in the areas of ethics and metaphysics. Israelite philosophers such as David and Solomon have made important contributions to the history of philosophy.

Understanding the impact of Israelite thought and influence on the rest of the world requires a nuanced and context-specific approach, which takes into account historical, cultural, political, and economic factors, as well as the agency of individuals and groups in shaping the impact of Israelite culture and values.

It is important to recognize the diversity of Israelite thought and practice, as well as how Israelite communities have interacted with and influenced other cultures throughout history.

Adding A Wife To Your Family

Romanticism and the Hebraic frame of thought are two distinct cultural movements that emerged in different historical periods and regions of the world. While there may be some overlap in their values and beliefs, there are also significant cultural differences between them.

Romanticism was a cultural movement that emerged in Europe during the late 18th and early 19th centuries. It was characterized by a celebration of individualism, emotion, and imagination, and a rejection of the rationalism and industrialization of the Enlightenment era. Romantic artists and writers often explored themes such as nature, love, and the supernatural, and valued the expression of personal feelings and experiences in their work.

The Hebraic frame of thought, on the other hand, is a cultural tradition that emerged in ancient Israel and continues to influence Israelite thought and practice today. It is characterized by a focus on the relationship between God and humanity, the importance of moral and ethical values, and the centrality of community and family in daily life. Hebraic thought values the study and interpretation of religious texts, such as the Torah, and emphasizes the importance of living a life of purpose and meaning.

While both Romanticism and Hebraic thought place value on individual experience and emotion, there are significant differences between the two cultural movements. Romanticism tends to prioritize individualism and self-expression, while Hebraic thought emphasizes communal and familial relationships, as well as the study and interpretation of religious texts. Additionally, Romanticism often explores themes of the supernatural and the mysterious, while Hebraic thought is rooted in a monotheistic understanding of the world.

While there may be some cultural overlap between Romanticism and Hebraic thought, there are also significant differences in their values and beliefs, which reflect the distinct historical and cultural contexts in which they emerged.

We currently live in a world overrun by Western Influence, and by default, Romanticism. This is why it has been so difficult for Israelite people who find themselves still in the places of their captivity to realize the value and importance of their cultural practices.

Once you've got a full grasp on Romanticism, and what the Hebraic frame of thought is, you can begin to take power steps towards your vision of an expanded family and how to articulate your decision from a cultural perspective that resonates most with you.

Adding a wife to a family can be a significant change, but approaching it with open communication, mutual respect, and a willingness to make adjustments, can lead to a positive and enriching experience for everyone involved. It is important to be mindful of each other's needs and work together to create a welcoming and comfortable environment. Adjusting to a new family dynamic takes time and effort, but it can also be a rewarding process that strengthens the bonds between family members.

When adding a wife to your family, it is important to make the necessary adjustments to ensure that everyone can adapt to the changes positively and healthily. Here are some tips on how to make these adjustments:

1. **Communicate openly and honestly:** It is important to have open and honest communication with your wife and other family members about expectations, needs, and boundaries. Discuss how everyone can work together to make the transition as smooth as possible, and be willing to compromise and make adjustments as needed.
2. **Respect each other's individuality:** Your wife may have different values, beliefs, and interests than your family members. It is important to respect these differences and make an effort to understand and appreciate each other's individuality.
3. **Establish clear roles and responsibilities:** Discuss and establish clear roles and responsibilities for everyone in the family. This can include tasks such as household chores, childcare, and financial

responsibilities. Make sure that everyone has a clear understanding of their role and feels comfortable with the arrangement.

4. **Create a welcoming environment:** Make an effort to create a welcoming and comfortable environment for your wife. This can include decorating the home together, planning family outings, and creating traditions that include everyone in the family.

5. **Address conflicts proactively:** Conflicts may arise when adding a new member to the family. It is important to address these conflicts proactively and work together to find a solution that works for everyone. Seek the help of a therapist or mediator if needed.

6. **Be patient and flexible:** Adjusting to a new family dynamic takes time and patience. Be patient with yourself, your wife, and other family members. Be flexible and willing to make adjustments as needed to ensure that everyone feels comfortable and happy in the family.

7. **Recognize the impact of the change:** Adding a new member to the family is a significant change that can affect everyone in the household. It is important to recognize and acknowledge the impact of this change on yourself and your family members.

8. **Embrace the transition:** Rather than resisting or avoiding the transition, try to embrace it as an opportunity for growth and positive change. Look for ways to adapt and adjust to the new dynamic, and keep an open mind and positive attitude.

9. **Be prepared to make adjustments:** Adding a wife to your family may require making adjustments to your daily routine, family traditions, and other aspects of your life. Be prepared to make these adjustments and approach them with a willingness to compromise and make changes as needed.

10. **Seek support:** It can be helpful to seek support from family members, friends, or a therapist during the transition. Talking to others about your experiences and concerns can help you process your emotions and work through any challenges that arise.

11. **Practice self-care:** Adding a wife to your family can be stressful, and it is important to practice self-care to maintain your mental and

emotional well-being. This can include activities such as exercise, meditation, spending time in nature, or engaging in hobbies that you enjoy.

12. **Focus on the positives:** While adding a wife to your family may come with challenges, it is important to focus on the positives and the potential benefits of the new dynamic. This can include the opportunity to create new traditions, deepen relationships, and experience personal growth.

Adding a wife to your family can be a challenging transition, but with open communication, mutual respect, and a willingness to make adjustments, it can be a positive and enriching experience for everyone involved.

It's important to also note that when adding a wife to your family, it is crucial to prepare your mindset for significant change.

By preparing your mindset for significant change when adding a wife to your family, you can approach the transition with a positive and resilient attitude. Embracing the change, being prepared to make adjustments, seeking support, practicing self-care, and focusing on the positives can help you navigate this transition successfully and create a happy and healthy family dynamic.

15

HOW TO BE PATIENT WITH YOUR WIFE

Patience Truly Is A Virtue

B eing patient can help you navigate difficult situations with grace, maintain a positive outlook in the face of challenges, and build stronger relationships with those around you.

In today's fast-paced world, it can be easy to become frustrated or overwhelmed when things don't go according to plan. However, cultivating patience can help you stay calm and focused, even when things are difficult or uncertain. It can also help you be more understanding and compassionate towards others, which can deepen your relationships and make you a better spouse, friend, and family member.

Moreover, patience is an important component of personal growth and development. When you're patient with yourself, you give yourself time to learn and grow at your own pace, without becoming discouraged by setbacks or mistakes. This can help you build resilience, confidence, and a stronger sense of self.

Being patient is a valuable skill that can help you navigate life's ups and downs with greater ease and grace. Whether you're working on developing more patience in your relationships, or simply trying to be more patient with yourself, it's a skill that's well worth cultivating.

Patience is a valuable skill in any relationship, whether it's a marriage or a friendship. It involves being able to tolerate and accept the imperfections and shortcomings of the other person, as well as being able to communicate calmly and respectfully even in difficult situations.

To cultivate patience in a relationship, it's important to first acknowledge that patience is a skill that requires practice and effort. It's not something that comes naturally to everyone, but it can be developed over time through intentional effort and practice.

This means being aware of your tendencies towards impatience, and actively working to develop greater patience over time. It's important to be patient with yourself as you work on this skill, and to celebrate small victories along the way.

One way to cultivate patience in a relationship is to practice mindfulness. This involves staying present at the moment and paying attention to your thoughts and feelings without judgment. When you're mindful, you're less likely to react impulsively or get swept up in negative emotions. Instead, you can take a step back and respond to the situation in a calm, rational manner.

Another way to cultivate patience in a relationship is to practice empathy. This involves putting yourself in your spouse's shoes and trying to see things from their perspective. When you can understand where your spouse is coming from, you're more likely to be patient with them and respond in a compassionate, understanding way.

It's important to remember that patience takes time and effort to develop. It's not something that happens overnight, but with consistent practice and effort, you can become more patient and understanding in your relationships. So, be patient with yourself and your spouse as you work on this skill, and celebrate the progress you make along the way.

Practicing patience requires us to work on becoming more self-aware of our own emotions and reactions. If you find yourself getting frustrated or angry with your spouse, take a moment to pause and reflect on why you're feeling that way. Are you reacting to something specific they did or said, or is it a deeper issue that needs to be addressed? By being more aware of your own emotions, you can learn to manage them better and respond to your spouse more patiently and compassionately.

Another important aspect of cultivating patience in a relationship is communication. It's important to communicate openly and honestly with your spouse, but also to listen actively and empathetically. When you're able to truly understand your spouse's perspective and feelings, it can be easier to be patient with them and work together to overcome challenges.

Finally, it's important to remember that patience is not just about tolerating the negatives in a relationship, but also about celebrating and appreciating the positives. Make an effort to express gratitude and appreciation for your spouse, and to focus on the things that make your relationship strong and fulfilling. This can help you stay motivated to continue practicing patience, even when things get tough.

My Wife Doesn't Understand My Goals

It can be frustrating when you feel like your wife isn't on the same page as you, especially when it comes to something as important as family goals.

One possible approach you could take is to have an open and honest conversation with your wife about your concerns. It's important to approach the conversation in a non-confrontational way and to be willing to listen to her perspective as well. Try to find a time when you're both calm and relaxed and make it clear that you want to have a constructive conversation.

Start by expressing how you feel and what your goals are for your family. Be specific about what you hope to achieve and why it's important to you. Then, give your wife a chance to respond and share her thoughts and feelings. Try to listen actively and empathetically, and avoid interrupting or dismissing her viewpoint.

Once you've both had a chance to share your perspectives, see if you can find common ground or a compromise that works for both of you. It may be helpful to break down your goals into smaller, more manageable steps that you can work on together.

Remember, communication and understanding are essential components of any healthy and successful relationship. By taking the time to listen to each other and work together towards shared goals, you can strengthen your relationship and build a brighter future for your family. Here are some tips and best practices on how to be patient with your wife:

1. **Practice empathy:** Try to put yourself in your wife's shoes and understand her perspective. Ask her questions and listen actively

to her responses. This will help you see things from her point of view and be more patient with her.

2. **Communicate openly:** Make sure that you communicate clearly and honestly with your wife. Be willing to share your thoughts and feelings, and ask her to do the same. When you're both on the same page, it's easier to be patient with each other.

3. **Practice mindfulness:** When you find yourself feeling frustrated or impatient, take a moment to breathe deeply and focus on the present moment. This can help you calm down and avoid overreacting.

4. **Set realistic expectations:** It's important to have realistic expectations of your wife, as well as yourself. Remember that no one is perfect, and everyone makes mistakes. Be patient with each other as you work towards your goals.

5. **Show appreciation:** Make an effort to show your wife that you appreciate her, and the things she does for you and your family. When you focus on the positive aspects of your relationship, it's easier to be patient with each other during difficult times.

6. **Take a break:** Sometimes, it's best to take a step back and give each other some space. If you're feeling frustrated or overwhelmed, take a break and do something that makes you happy. When you come back to the situation, you may find that you have a renewed sense of patience and understanding.

Being patient with your wife is an ongoing process, and it takes time and effort. By practicing empathy, communicating openly, and showing appreciation, you can strengthen your relationship and build a deeper sense of understanding and trust.

When spouses take the time to actively listen to each other and work together towards common goals, they can build a strong foundation of trust, respect, and love.

Effective communication involves not just talking, but also active listening.

It's important to listen to your wife's thoughts, feelings, and concerns without interrupting or dismissing them. When you show empathy and understanding, your spouse feels heard and valued, which strengthens your bond.

Furthermore, working together towards shared goals can be a powerful way to deepen your connection and build a brighter future for your family. By setting and achieving goals together, you can build a sense of teamwork and mutual support. It's important to remember that every relationship has its ups and downs, but by communicating openly and working together, you can overcome challenges and build a strong, fulfilling relationship.

So, if you're looking to strengthen your relationship with your wife, remember to prioritize communication and understanding. Take the time to listen to each other, share your thoughts and feelings openly, and work together towards shared goals. With patience, commitment, and love, you can build a successful, fulfilling relationship that lasts a lifetime.

16

HOW TO MAINTAIN A SOLID RELATIONSHIP WITH YOUR CHILDREN AS THE FAMILY EXPANDS

The proof is in the pudding and cannot be emphasized enough: maintaining a solid relationship with your children as the family expands is of the utmost importance. In this chapter we will cover some information, along with helpful insights, to assist you in keeping the relationships with your children fortified and strong.

It is essential to establish a strong emotional bond with your children from an early age. As children grow, their emotions develop and evolve, and it is crucial to address these changes to foster a healthy and trusting relationship. If you are a father, this essential emotional bond will need to be established well before you decide to expand upon your existing family dynamics.

Expanding your family without addressing the emotional needs of your children will be a cause of great frustration and unneeded friction amongst all members of your Divine Family Unit. Children need to know they are appreciated, loved, and valued members of the family.

If you place the pursuit of family expansion ahead of ensuring that your children are emotionally stable, they will assume that you care for and love your new wife more than you do them.

If your new wife already has children, you will have to exercise even more sensitivity regarding your children because they will grow resentful towards you, your new wife, and her children if you spend more quality time with them, or if you show preferential treatment towards them in an attempt to acclimate them into your foundational family. You also run the risk of illustrating a lack of balance and equality in pertinence to your time-management skills.

As the family expands, the dynamics and routines change and it may become challenging to keep up with the emotional needs of your children. However, making time for your children, actively listening to them, and being emotionally present can go a long way in maintaining a strong relationship.

It is also essential to understand that each child is unique and may have different emotional needs. Therefore, it is crucial to address these needs on an individual basis and provide the necessary support and guidance. Children appreciate the thoughtful little things that parents do for them. In regards to an expanded family dynamic, time is the most valued resource you will have.

There are so many smaller elements that make up the foundation for a successful Divine Family Unit. Take the time to truly familiarize yourself with as many different aspects of this journey as possible, and be willing to learn new methods and techniques for leading your family constantly. You will also need to be patient with yourself as you expand the way you think and process information.

Maintaining a solid relationship with your children as the family expands is critical for their emotional development, understanding, and growth. It can help build trust, strengthen communication, and foster a sense of security and belonging in the family.

Many children won't initially know how to process their father having another wife while still being married to their mom and may want to grow closer to her in an attempt to console her if they feel that she is sad about your decision to expand your family. Whatever you do, don't let this deter you from establishing that important bond with them. It will take extra effort and work from you, but the result will be well worth the energy you put into them, as long as you stay determined to see your vision thru.

As the family expands, there will be more demands on your time and attention, but it is just as crucial to prioritize spending quality time with your children as it is to spend quality time with your wives. This means carving out time in your schedule to engage in activities together, such as playing games, reading books, or simply having meaningful conversations.

Actively listening to your children is also essential. This means giving them your full attention when they are speaking and being open and receptive to their thoughts and feelings. It is essential to validate their emotions, even if you do not agree with their perspective, as it helps them feel heard and understood.

The biggest issues that families face are usually rooted in a lack of transparent communication between family members, and the emotional fallout that derives from the feelings of not being heard or appreciated.

Being emotionally present means being attuned to your children's emotional needs and responding appropriately. This includes providing comfort and support when they are upset or celebrating their achievements and successes.

Children usually show gratitude by doing their chores when asked, without complaining, or working diligently in their school studies. They foster better relationships between themselves and tend to be more creative in their thinking when they feel appreciated by their parents, especially their father. You would be wise to keep in mind, as a rule of thumb, that when a child feels appreciated, they will also show appreciation.

Remember that children will imitate and do what they see before they do what they are told. Make sure that you are an exemplary example of a man, husband, and father in the lives of them and their mothers as you continue expanding your Divine Family Unit.

Hopefully, you've come to see that cultivating a strong relationship with your children as the family expands requires making time for them, actively listening to them, and being emotionally present. By doing so, you can build a strong and healthy relationship that will benefit your family for years to come.

Furthermore, establishing a solid relationship with your children as the family expands can be challenging, but it is essential for a happy and healthy family. Here are some best practices to help you maintain a strong relationship with your children:

1. **Spend quality time with your children:** Set aside some time each day to spend with your children. It doesn't have to be anything fancy or expensive; even just reading a book together or going for a walk can help you connect with your children.
2. **Be present:** When you are with your children, be present at the moment. Put down your phone, turn off the TV, and listen to what they have to say.
3. **Create traditions:** Establish traditions that your family can look forward to and enjoy together. This can be something as simple as a

weekly family movie night or a monthly game night. Eventually, you will want to create new traditions that include your new wife and your children. This can help everyone feel more connected and included.

4. **Involve your children in decision-making:** Involve your children in decisions that affect the family. This will make them feel valued and important, and it will also help them learn important decision-making skills.

5. **Show affection:** Show your children affection regularly, whether it is through hugs, kisses, or kind words. This will help them feel loved and secure.

6. **Stay consistent:** Be consistent in your parenting approach, and make sure that both parents are on the same page. This will help your children feel more secure and confident.

7. **Prioritize communication:** Prioritize open and honest communication with your children. Encourage them to express their thoughts and feelings, and validate their emotions.

Spending quality time with your children is essential for building a strong, loving relationship and helping them feel valued and cared for. And you're right, it doesn't have to be anything elaborate or costly.

Even small, simple activities like playing a game, doing a craft, cooking a meal together, or even just sitting and chatting can make a big difference in how connected you feel to your children.

The key is to make a conscious effort to set aside time every day, even if it's just 15-20 minutes, to focus solely on your children and give them your undivided attention. This can be especially important in today's busy world where there are so many distractions and demands on our time.

Spending quality time with your children now will have a lasting impact on their lives and the relationship you have with them. So, make it a priority and enjoy the special moments you share!

Being present and fully engaged when you're spending time with your children is key to building a strong, healthy relationship with them.

This means setting aside distractions and giving your children your undivided attention. Turning off the TV, putting down your phone, and actively listening to what they have to say can make a big difference in how connected you feel to each other.

It can be all too easy to get caught up in the busyness of life and forget to be fully present at the moment. But when you take the time to tune in to your children and show them that you care about what they have to say, you're sending them a powerful message that they are important to you.

In addition to being a great way to strengthen your relationship with your children, being present at the moment can also be a powerful stress reliever. When you're fully engaged with your children and not distracted by other things, you're more likely to feel calm and centered, which can help you recharge and feel more energized.

Making an effort to be present and engaged when you're spending time with your children will reward you in ways that you may have never thought of. You'll be amazed at how much more connected and fulfilled you both will feel.

Involving children in family decisions is a great way to show them that their opinions and ideas matter and can help them develop important life skills.

It's important to give children a voice and a sense of agency in family decision-making, even if the final decision rests with the parents. This can help them feel more invested in the outcome and can be a great way to teach them about collaboration, negotiation, and problem-solving.

Some creative ways to involve children in family decisions might include:

- Asking for their input on family activities, outings, or vacations

- Encouraging them to share their thoughts on household rules or routines

- Letting them help with planning and organizing family events or celebrations

- Involving them in decisions about household purchases or budgeting

By involving your children in decisions that affect the family, you're helping to foster their sense of independence, responsibility, and ownership in the family dynamic. This can go a long way in building a positive and respectful relationship between parents and children and can help children feel more confident and competent as they grow and develop.

Showing affection to your children is a great way to help them feel loved, valued, and secure. This can be especially important during times of stress, change, or uncertainty.

There are many ways to show affection to your children, and what works best will depend on your child's personality and preferences. Some children may love to be hugged and cuddled, while others may prefer more verbal expressions of affection, such as kind words or affirmations.

Regularly expressing affection can help build a strong emotional bond between parents and children, which can have positive effects on many areas of a child's life, including their self-esteem, social skills, and emotional resilience.

Here are some tips for showing affection to your children:

- **Be spontaneous:** Don't wait for a special occasion to show your children affection. Make it a regular part of your interactions, whether it's a hug before bedtime or a kind word of encouragement before a big test.

- **Tailor your approach:** Some children may be more receptive to physical affection, while others may prefer verbal expressions of love and support. Pay attention to your child's cues and adjust your approach accordingly. There are plenty of resources dedicated to learning a person's Love Language, and it would be well worth your efforts to look into some of them.

- **Be consistent:** Make showing affection a regular part of your family culture. This can help children feel secure and loved, even during times of stress or uncertainty.

- **Be mindful of your child's boundaries:** While showing affection is important, it's also important to respect your child's boundaries and preferences. If your child doesn't want to be hugged or kissed, find other ways to show your love and support.

Helping your children feel loved and secure by showing affection to them is a powerful way to tighten the bond between you. Make it a regular part of your interactions, and watch your relationship with your child grow stronger every day!

As dads and husbands, it's imperative that we put effort into showing up for our family every day. The vision to expand your family was given to you, and not your wife or wives. Even if your wife makes mention of you marrying another woman, she will be relying on your vision to reach the desired outcome.

Consistency in parenting is key to providing children with a sense of stability, security, and predictability. When parents are on the same page and have a consistent approach to parenting, children feel more confident and secure in their environment, which can have a positive impact on their behavior and emotional well-being.

Here are some tips for maintaining consistency in your parenting approach:

- **Establish clear expectations and boundaries:** Communicate your expectations and boundaries to your children, and consistently enforce them.

- **Be on the same page as your co-parent:** Make sure both parents are on the same page when it comes to parenting decisions and discipline. This can help avoid confusion and conflict and can help ensure that your children receive consistent messages and expectations from both parents.

- **Be consistent with consequences:** When your child breaks a rule or boundary, be consistent with the consequences. This can help your child understand that there are consequences for their actions and can help reinforce the importance of following rules and boundaries.

- **Listen to your child's perspective:** While it's important to be consistent, it's also important to listen to your child's perspective and consider their feelings. This can help you make more informed decisions and can help your child feel heard and respected.

Consistency in parenting takes effort and communication, but it can have a positive impact on your child's development and emotional well-being. By establishing clear expectations, being on the same page as your co-parent, and being consistent with consequences, you can help your child feel more secure and confident in their environment.

Similarly, creating traditions with your children can also help to strengthen your bond. Traditions provide a sense of stability and continuity, and they also create memories that your family can look back on with fondness. Whether it's a holiday tradition, a special meal, or a weekly family activity, creating traditions can help to bring your family closer together and create a sense of belonging.

Lastly, communication is essential for building a strong and healthy relationship with your children. When you prioritize communication, you create a safe space where your children can share their thoughts and feelings with you, and this helps to build trust and connection.

As you begin to establish your Divine Family Unit, remember that it's common for children to feel apprehensive or uneasy when their dad marries another woman while still being married to their mother.

Societal pressures will be difficult to navigate if you allow your children to focus their attention on what everyone outside of your Divine Family Unit has to say regarding the family structure you're establishing. However, there are things you can do to reassure your children that everything will be okay:

1. **Validate their feelings and emotions:** Acknowledge your children's feelings and let them know that it's okay to feel apprehensive or uncertain. Reassure them that you understand their concerns and that you're here to support them. It's just as important to validate your child's emotions, even if you don't agree with their perspective. This can involve acknowledging their feelings, reflecting on what you've heard, and avoiding invalidating comments like "You shouldn't feel that way" or "That's not a big deal."

2. **Have an open and honest conversation:** Talk to your children about your new wife and the changes that are happening in the family. Encourage them to express their feelings and concerns, and listen to them without judgment.

3. **Involve your children in the process:** Involve your children in the wedding planning and preparations, if possible. This can help them feel more included and invested in the process.

4. **Spend quality time with your children:** Make sure to set aside quality time for your children, even after you get remarried. This will help reassure them that they are still a priority in your life.

5. **Be patient:** Give your children time to adjust to the changes in the family. It may take some time for them to feel comfortable with your new wife, but with patience and support, they will eventually come around.

6. **Create a safe space:** Make sure your children feel safe and comfortable sharing their thoughts and feelings with you. This can involve creating a non-judgmental and supportive environment, and avoiding criticism or blame when your child expresses their feelings.

7. **Encourage expression:** Encourage your children to express their thoughts and feelings in a way that feels comfortable for them. This may involve active listening, asking open-ended questions, or simply providing opportunities for your child to express themselves in a safe and supportive environment.

8. **Model open communication:** Show your children that open communication is important by modeling it yourself. This can involve sharing your thoughts and feelings, being honest and transparent, and acknowledging your own mistakes or shortcomings.

Prioritizing open and honest communication with your children takes effort and patience, but it can have a positive impact on your relationship and their overall development.

By creating a safe space, encouraging expression, validating emotions, and modeling open communication, you can help your children develop strong communication skills and emotional intelligence, which can serve them well throughout their lives, and not just within your Divine Family Unit.

There is no need to regret your decision to expand your family when things occasionally get difficult to deal with. Showcase your abilities to be an effective leader by implementing the best practices in this chapter whenever you feel a sense of unsurety about the relationships you have with your children.

Always remember how important it is to be sensitive to your children's feelings during this transition period. By being patient, understanding, and supportive, you can help your children feel more comfortable with your new wife and create a happy and harmonious family dynamic.

Maintaining a strong relationship with your children requires effort, time, and commitment. But the rewards are immeasurable, and it will help create a happy and healthy family.

17

LEARNING TO LISTEN TO YOUR WIFE'S CONCERNS AND RESPONDING WITH WISDOM

I n the busyness of life, it's easy to neglect communication with your spouse. However, making time to listen to your wife's concerns and prioritizing your communication is crucial for maintaining a strong and healthy marriage.

One way to ensure that you're making time for your wife is to set aside specific times each day or week to talk. This could mean having a regular weekly date night or simply making a habit of checking in with each other at the end of each day. Whatever approach you take, it's important to make sure that you're fully present and engaged during those conversations.

When you're talking with your wife, try to eliminate distractions and focus your attention solely on her. This means putting away your phone or other electronic devices and giving her your undivided attention. This will help her feel heard and valued, and show her that you're committed to your relationship.

Effective communication, active listening, and understanding are essential to maintaining a strong and healthy marriage. By taking the time to listen to your wife's concerns and responding with wisdom, you can create a safe and supportive environment where she feels valued and heard. This, in turn, can help to strengthen the bond between you and your wife and lead to a more fulfilling and rewarding relationship.

Remember, marriage is a partnership, and by working together and prioritizing communication, you can overcome any challenges and enjoy a lifetime of love and happiness.

Marriage also requires effective communication, active listening, and understanding. As a husband, one of the most important things you can do to foster a healthy and happy marriage is to learn to listen to your wife's concerns and respond with wisdom.

Here are some key tips and best practices to help you become a better listener and respond to your wife's concerns with wisdom:

1. **Make time to listen:** It's easy to get caught up in the busyness of life and neglect to listen to your wife's concerns. However, it's important to make time for her and prioritize your communication. Set aside specific times each day or week to talk, and make sure you're fully present and engaged during those conversations.
2. **Be present:** When your wife is talking to you, give her your full attention. Put down your phone or turn off the TV, and focus on what she's saying. Make eye contact, nod, and use active listening skills to show her that you're engaged and interested.
3. **Validate her feelings:** If your wife is sharing a concern or issue with you, it's important to validate her feelings. Acknowledge that her concerns are valid and that you understand how she's feeling. This will help her feel heard and validated, which is key to building trust

and intimacy in your relationship.

4. **Practice empathy:** Empathy is the ability to understand and share someone else's feelings. Put yourself in your wife's shoes and try to see things from her perspective. This will help you respond with compassion and wisdom, rather than defensiveness or anger.

5. **Don't try to fix everything:** As men, we often want to fix problems and find solutions quickly. However, sometimes our wives just need us to listen and validate their feelings. Don't rush to offer solutions or try to fix everything right away. Sometimes, the best thing you can do is just be there for your wife and offer support.

6. **Respond with wisdom:** Once you've listened to your wife's concerns and validated her feelings, it's important to respond with wisdom. This means taking a thoughtful and measured approach to problem-solving. Consider all of the options and consequences before making a decision, and make sure that your response is in line with your values and your commitment to your wife.

Effective communication is the foundation of a strong and healthy marriage. By making time for your wife, prioritizing your communication, and being fully present and engaged during those conversations, you can build a deeper, more meaningful connection with your spouse, and enjoy a happier, more fulfilling marriage.

It's important to understand that sometimes, your wife may not be looking for a solution to her problem, but rather just needs someone to listen to her and validate her feelings. Rushing to offer solutions can sometimes come across as dismissive of her concerns or feelings, and may make her feel unheard or undervalued.

Instead, try to focus on actively listening to your wife and providing emotional support. This means being present, empathizing with her feelings, and offering words of encouragement or affirmation. Let her know that you're there for her and that you care about her, and be willing to simply sit with her and listen, without judgment or criticism.

By providing this kind of support and validation, you can help your wife feel more secure and connected in your relationship, and strengthen your bond as a couple. Remember, sometimes the best way to support your partner is simply to be there for them, listen to them, and offer your love and support.

Empathy is a crucial component of effective communication and building a strong relationship with your wife. By putting yourself in her shoes and trying to see things from her perspective, you can gain a deeper understanding of her feelings, needs, and concerns.

This can help you respond with compassion and wisdom, rather than reacting defensively or with anger. It's important to remember that everyone has different experiences and perspectives, and what may seem insignificant or trivial to you may be a significant concern for your wife.

By showing empathy and taking the time to understand your wife's perspective, you can create a safe and supportive environment for her to express herself and feel heard. This, in turn, can help to build trust and intimacy in your relationship and lead to a more fulfilling and rewarding marriage.

Also, empathy is not just about understanding your wife's feelings, but also about showing her that you care and are willing to support her. By being empathetic and responsive to your wife's needs, you can strengthen your relationship and create a happier, more fulfilling life together.

Validation is a critical aspect of effective communication and building a strong relationship with your wife. When your wife shares a concern or issue with you, it's important to acknowledge her feelings and validate them. This means listening attentively to what she's saying, and showing her that you understand and care about how she's feeling.

By validating your wife's feelings, you can create a safe and supportive environment for her to express herself and feel heard. This can help to build trust and intimacy in your relationship and strengthen your bond as a couple.

Validation doesn't necessarily mean agreeing with everything your wife says or feels, but rather acknowledging and respecting her perspective. It's important to avoid dismissive or belittling language, and instead, focus on actively listening and empathizing with her.

Remember, validation is a powerful tool for building trust and intimacy in your relationship. By taking the time to listen and validate your wife's feelings, you can create a stronger, more fulfilling marriage.

Responding with wisdom is also a key component of effective communication in marriage. After listening to your wife's concerns and validating her feelings, it's important to take a thoughtful and measured approach to problem-solving.

This means considering all of the options and consequences before making a decision, and ensuring that your response is in line with your values and your commitment to your wife. It's important to approach problem-solving collaboratively and respectfully and to work together to find a solution that works for both of you.

In some cases, this may mean compromising or finding a middle ground that meets both of your needs. In other cases, it may mean taking a step back and re-evaluating the situation before making a decision. Whatever approach you take, it's important to remember that responding with wisdom requires patience, humility, and a willingness to learn and grow together as a couple.

By responding with wisdom, and working together to find solutions that meet both of your needs, you can build a deeper, more meaningful connection with your spouse, and enjoy a happier, more fulfilling marriage.

Learning to listen to your wife's concerns and responding with wisdom is a key component of a healthy and happy marriage. By making time to listen, being present, validating her feelings, practicing empathy, not trying to fix everything, and responding with wisdom, you can build a strong and meaningful connection with your wife that will last a lifetime.

18

LEARNING HOW TO MAXIMIZE YOUR TIME, AND BEING FLEXIBLE WITH YOUR SCHEDULE

P rioritizing your tasks and having a schedule are important aspects of maximizing your time, but it is equally important to be flexible. Unexpected events or emergencies can arise, and it's important to be prepared to adjust your schedule accordingly.

Being flexible means that you are open to changing your plans and adapting to new circumstances. It's important to be able to shift your priorities and schedule as needed to ensure that you can still accomplish your goals, even in the face of unexpected events. Being too rigid in your schedule can lead to stress and burnout, so it's important to find a balance between structure and flexibility.

Learning how to maximize your time and being flexible with your schedule are essential skills that can greatly enhance your productivity and overall well-being. In today's fast-paced world, it is easy to become overwhelmed by the sheer amount of tasks and responsibilities that we need to accomplish in a day. However, by adopting some simple strategies and adopting a flexible mindset, you can make the most of your time and achieve your goals with ease.

1. **Prioritize your tasks:** One of the most effective ways to maximize your time is by prioritizing your tasks. Make a list of everything you need to accomplish in a day, and then rank them in order of importance. Focus on completing the most important tasks first, as they are usually the ones that will have the biggest impact on your overall productivity.

2. **Create a schedule:** Having a schedule is key to maximizing your time. Set aside specific times for different tasks, and stick to them as much as possible. This will help you stay on track and ensure that you don't waste time on less important activities.

3. **Be flexible:** While having a schedule is important, it is also essential to be flexible. Unexpected events or emergencies can disrupt your plans, so it is crucial to have a backup plan in place. If something unexpected comes up, be prepared to adjust your schedule accordingly.

4. **Learn to say no:** It can be tempting to take on too much and try to do everything at once. However, this can quickly lead to burnout and decreased productivity. Learn to say no to tasks that are not essential or can be done at a later time.

5. **Eliminate distractions:** Distractions can be a major time-waster. Identify the things that distract you the most and take steps to eliminate them. This may involve turning off your phone, closing your email, or finding a quiet space to work.

6. **Take breaks:** Taking regular breaks is essential for maintaining productivity and avoiding burnout. Schedule some downtime throughout your day, and use this time to recharge your batteries and relax.

7. **Use technology:** There are many tools and apps available that can help you maximize your time and stay on track. Consider using a task management app, a calendar app, or a time-tracking tool to help you stay organized and focused.

Before considering expanding your family, you must learn how to maximize your time and be flexible with your schedule. Learning these skills is essential for achieving your goals and living a balanced life.

By adopting some simple strategies and adopting a flexible mindset, you can make the most of your time and accomplish your tasks with ease. Remember to prioritize your tasks, create a schedule, be flexible, eliminate distractions, take breaks, and use technology to help you stay organized and focused.

Learning how to maximize your time and being flexible with your schedule is especially important when leading your family. As a leader, you likely have many responsibilities and tasks to accomplish, including taking care of your family's needs, managing your household, and perhaps even balancing a career or other commitments.

By prioritizing your tasks and creating a schedule, you can ensure that you are making the most of your time and staying on track with your responsibilities. This can help you to be more efficient and effective in your role as a leader, allowing you to better meet the needs of your family.

However, it's also important to be flexible when leading your family. Unexpected events, such as a child becoming sick or a family emergency, can quickly disrupt even the most well-planned schedule. In these situations, being flexible and able to adapt to changing circumstances is crucial.

As a leader, it's important to model this flexibility for your family as well. This means being open to changing plans and adapting to new circumstances when necessary. It also means being willing to delegate tasks and responsibilities to other family members when needed.

By learning how to maximize your time and being flexible with your schedule, you can become a more effective and successful leader for your family. This can help you to create a happier and more harmonious household, while also allowing you to balance your other commitments and responsibilities outside of the home.

Learning how to maximize your time and being flexible with your schedule is also crucial for managing multiple family members and avoiding burnout. When you have a family to manage, you likely have a lot of responsibilities to juggle, including caring for children, managing household chores, and possibly even holding down a job.

By prioritizing your tasks and creating a schedule, you can ensure that you are making the most of your time and staying on track with your responsibilities. This can help you to be more efficient and effective in your role as a caregiver, allowing you to better meet the needs of your family members.

At the same time, being flexible is also important when managing a family. Unexpected events can quickly disrupt even the most well-planned schedule, and being able to adapt to changing circumstances is crucial. This means being willing to shift your priorities, adjust your schedule, and delegate tasks to others when needed.

By learning how to balance structure and flexibility in your approach to managing your family, you can avoid becoming overwhelmed or burned out. You can stay level-headed, even when unexpected events arise, and you can better manage your responsibilities without sacrificing your well-being. This can help you create a happier and more harmonious household, which can benefit everyone in your family.

Maximizing your time and being flexible with your schedule can have a significant impact on your overall well-being and quality of life. When you have a clear plan and structure in place for managing your time, you can be more productive and accomplish more with less stress.

By prioritizing your tasks and creating a schedule, you can ensure that you are making the most of your time and staying on track with your goals. This can help you to feel more in control and less overwhelmed by your responsibilities. Additionally, being flexible and adaptable can help you to better manage unexpected events or changes in your plans, which can reduce stress and anxiety.

Overall, by learning how to maximize your time and be flexible with your schedule, you can create a more balanced and fulfilling life. You can achieve your goals without sacrificing your well-being, and you can approach each day with greater clarity and confidence.

Congratulations on making this positive change in your life!

19

BEING A LEADER WHILE MAINTAINING ORDER AND DISCIPLINE IN YOUR HOUSEHOLD

Being a leader while maintaining order and discipline in your household is important for several reasons. Firstly, it helps to create a stable and predictable environment where family members know what is expected of them and what the consequences are for breaking the rules. This can lead to fewer conflicts and a more peaceful household.

Secondly, it can help to promote a sense of responsibility and accountability among family members, as they know that their actions have consequences. Thirdly, it can help to foster respect and trust between family members, as they know that the rules apply equally to everyone and that they can rely on each other to follow them.

As a leader in your household, you can model positive behavior and set an example for your family members to follow. You can communicate your expectations, enforce the rules consistently and fairly, and use positive reinforcement to encourage good behavior.

You can also encourage open communication and work with your family members to find solutions to any problems that arise. By being a leader and maintaining order and discipline in your household, you can create a positive and supportive environment that promotes respect, trust, and cooperation among family members.

Modeling the behavior you want to see in others is a crucial aspect of leadership. When you exhibit respectful and kind behavior, you set an example for your family members to follow. Children, in particular, learn from their parent's behavior, so it's important to model positive behaviors that you want your children to emulate.

By showing respect and kindness to your family members, you demonstrate that these behaviors are valued and important in your household. This, in turn, can encourage your family members to exhibit similar behaviors towards each other, creating a more positive and harmonious home environment.

Clear communication of expectations is essential when establishing rules and maintaining order in your household. When you communicate your expectations clearly, you leave little room for confusion or misunderstandings. It's important to explain why certain rules are in place and how they benefit the entire family.

Additionally, it's important to make sure that the rules are fair and reasonable. This means that the consequences for not meeting those expectations should be appropriate and proportionate to the behavior.

When everyone in the household understands the rules and the consequences of not following them, it creates a sense of accountability and responsibility for their actions, which can lead to better behavior and fewer conflicts.

Consistency is crucial in maintaining order and discipline in your household. When you enforce the rules consistently, it sends a clear message to your family members that you are serious about maintaining order and that everyone is held accountable for their actions.

Consistency also helps to establish trust and respect between family members because they know that the rules apply equally to everyone in the household. It's also essential to apply consequences fairly across the board, meaning that the consequences should be the same for everyone who breaks the rules. This ensures that everyone is treated fairly and that there is no favoritism or bias in the household.

When you consistently enforce the rules and apply consequences fairly, it creates a sense of stability and predictability in your household, which can lead to better behavior and fewer conflicts.

Praising and rewarding good behavior is an effective way to encourage and motivate family members to continue following the rules and exhibiting positive behavior. Positive reinforcement is a powerful tool that can help to create a positive and supportive environment in your household.

When you praise and reward good behavior, you are sending a message to your family members that their actions are appreciated and valued. This, in turn, can lead to an increase in that behavior, as people tend to repeat behaviors that are rewarded. Some examples of rewards could be verbal praise, a special treat, extra privileges, or a small gift.

The rewards don't have to be big or expensive, but they should be meaningful and demonstrate that you recognize and appreciate their efforts. By using positive reinforcement, you can create a more positive and supportive household environment, where family members feel motivated to follow the rules and exhibit good behavior.

It's important to be firm in enforcing the rules, but also be fair and reasonable in your approach. While it's important to hold your family members accountable for their actions, using harsh punishment or discipline can harm your relationship with them and create an atmosphere of fear or resentment. Instead, focus on consequences that are proportionate to the behavior and help to teach a lesson, rather than just punishing.

When you approach discipline calmly and reasonably, it sends a message that you care about your family member's well-being and want to help them learn from their mistakes. This can lead to a stronger relationship built on trust and respect.

Remember to take into account each family member's age and individual needs when deciding on consequences, and be open to hearing their perspective and allowing for discussion. By being firm but fair in your approach to discipline, you can help to maintain order and respect in your household while also building stronger relationships with your family members.

As the head of the household, it's essential to maintain order and discipline to create a harmonious and comfortable living environment for everyone. Here are some tips and best practices on how to be a leader while maintaining order and discipline in your household:

1. **Lead by example:** As a leader, you must model the behavior you want to see in your family members. If you want them to be respectful and kind, then you must show them respect and kindness.
2. **Set clear expectations:** Communicate your expectations clearly and explain the consequences of not meeting those expectations. Ensure that everyone understands the rules and that they are fair and reasonable.
3. **Consistency:** Consistency is critical in maintaining order and dis-

cipline. Make sure that you enforce the rules consistently and apply consequences fairly across the board.

4. **Use positive reinforcement:** When family members follow the rules or exhibit good behavior, praise and reward them. Positive reinforcement is an effective way to encourage and motivate people to continue doing the right thing.

5. **Be firm but fair:** It's important to be firm in enforcing the rules but also be fair and reasonable. Avoid using harsh punishment or discipline that may harm your relationship with your family members.

6. **Encourage open communication:** Encourage your family members to communicate openly with you. Listen to their concerns and suggestions, and work together to find solutions to any problems that arise.

Being a leader while maintaining order and discipline in your household requires consistency, clear communication, positive reinforcement, fairness, and open communication. By implementing these strategies, you can create a respectful and harmonious living environment for everyone in your household.

Encouraging open communication with your family members is essential to maintaining a positive and healthy household. By creating an environment where everyone feels comfortable expressing their thoughts and feelings, you can help to prevent conflicts and build stronger relationships.

When family members feel heard and valued, they are more likely to cooperate and work together towards a common goal. To encourage open communication, make sure that you are approachable and available to listen to your family members' concerns and suggestions.

When someone comes to you with a problem, take the time to listen actively and try to understand their perspective.

Ask questions and offer support to help them find a solution that works for everyone. Additionally, make sure that you model good communication skills by being respectful and non-judgmental in your responses.

By working together and communicating openly, you can create a household that is built on mutual respect, trust, and cooperation.

20

SINGLE MOTHERHOOD IS AT AN ALL-TIME HIGH

Single Motherhood Is Not Slowing Down

Single motherhood is indeed at an all-time high in the United States, with more than 80% of single-parent households being headed by women. While some of these women are divorced or widowed, a significant portion are never-married mothers who are raising their children on their own. This trend has important implications for the well-being of both mothers and children, as well as for society as a whole.

The reasons behind the rise in single motherhood are complex and multifaceted. Economic factors play a major role, with many women struggling to make ends meet and facing limited opportunities for stable employment. The decline of marriage as a social institution and the increasing acceptance of non-traditional family structures are also factors that have contributed to the rise in single motherhood.

Whatever the reasons behind this trend, it is clear that single mothers face unique challenges that can make it difficult to provide for themselves and their children. Single mothers are more likely to live in poverty, struggle with debt, and lack access to healthcare and other necessities. They also face higher rates of depression and other mental health problems.

Fortunately, there are steps that we can take as a society to help support single mothers and their families. One key area where action is needed is in the realm of public policy. We need to ensure that single mothers have access to affordable housing, quality healthcare, and job training programs that can help them build a stable future for themselves and their children.

Another important step is to address the root causes of single motherhood, such as poverty and economic inequality. We need to work towards creating a more just and equitable society that provides opportunities for all individuals to succeed, regardless of their race, gender, or socioeconomic background.

Finally, we need to work to change the cultural norms and attitudes that contribute to the stigmatization of single mothers. Single motherhood should not be seen as a failure or a moral failing, but rather as a difficult but important choice that many women make to provide for their families.

The rise in single motherhood is a complex and multifaceted issue that requires a comprehensive response from policymakers, social service providers, and the broader community. By taking steps to support single mothers and address the root causes of single motherhood, we can help ensure that all families have the resources they need to thrive.

Cultural togetherness and community support are essential in helping single mothers navigate the challenges of raising children on their own. By creating a sense of belonging and social support, cultural communities can help alleviate the feelings of isolation and loneliness that often accompany single parenthood. This, in turn, can help reduce the risk of depression and anxiety that single mothers may face.

Cultural communities provide a unique opportunity for single mothers to connect with others who share similar values, experiences, and traditions. This can create a sense of solidarity and belonging that is often missing in other areas of their lives. For example, single mothers may be able to connect with other single mothers from their cultural community who have similar experiences of navigating the challenges of raising children on their own.

In addition to providing social support, cultural communities can also offer practical assistance to single mothers. For example, members of the community may be able to help with childcare, transportation, or other needs. This can be especially important for single mothers who may not have access to extended family support or who are struggling financially.

It is also important to note that cultural communities can play a role in reducing the stigma and negative attitudes toward single motherhood. By creating a culture of acceptance and support, cultural communities can help combat the societal messages that single motherhood is a failure or a moral failing.

However, it is important to recognize that not all cultural communities may be equally supportive of single mothers. Some communities may hold traditional gender roles that emphasize marriage and family structure, which can lead to negative attitudes toward single mothers. Cultural communities need to challenge these stereotypes and create an inclusive environment that supports all members, regardless of their family structure.

When you think about it, cultural togetherness and community support can be powerful tools in helping single mothers navigate the challenges of parenthood. By providing social support, practical assistance, and a sense of belonging, cultural communities can help reduce the risk of depression and anxiety that often accompany single parenthood.

It is important for cultural communities to challenge negative attitudes toward single motherhood and to create an inclusive environment that supports all members.

Joining A Loving, Expanding Family

While polygyny, the practice of one man having multiple wives, may provide some benefits for single mothers, it is important to consider the potential drawbacks.

When identifying whether or not joining an expanding family is for you, it is important that you are made aware of the fact that polygynous families may face challenges in terms of emotional and financial resources. The husband may struggle to provide equally for all of his wives and their children, which can lead to unequal treatment and resentment among family members.

Single mothers who join a polygynous family may find themselves competing for resources and attention with the other wives and their children.

It is also important to consider the potential impact on the children involved in a polygynous family. Children may struggle with feelings of insecurity and uncertainty in a family structure that is not widely accepted or recognized. They may also face challenges in developing strong relationships with their father, as he may not be able to provide equal time and attention to all of his children.

However, joining a loving family can certainly offer single mothers and their children the opportunity to build a stable foundation, and it may provide an alternative to the societal stigma associated with single motherhood. However, it is important to consider the ethical implications and potential challenges of this option.

Firstly, it is important to ensure that the family is a safe and healthy environment for both the mother and her children. It is essential to conduct thorough background checks and ensure that the family is not engaging in any abusive or harmful behaviors.

Additionally, joining a new family can be a difficult transition for both the mother and her children. It is important to ensure that the family is supportive and welcoming and that the mother and children can develop strong relationships with their new family members.

Furthermore, it is important to consider the impact on the children's sense of identity and attachment. Children who are adopted or who join a new family may struggle with feelings of abandonment or loss, and it is important to provide them with the support and resources they need to process these emotions.

Moreover, it is important to recognize that not all families may be willing or able to take on the responsibilities of raising someone else's children. It is essential to approach this option with sensitivity and respect for the family's needs and boundaries.

Several steps can be taken to assist women dealing with single motherhood, which is indeed at an all-time high. Here are some suggestions:

1. **Financial Support:** Single mothers often face financial struggles due to the lack of support from a partner. Providing financial assistance such as affordable housing, food assistance, and childcare subsidies can help alleviate some of the financial burdens they face.

2. **Education and Job Training:** Many single mothers struggle to find employment that allows them to support their families. Providing education and job training opportunities can help them gain the skills and knowledge needed to secure better-paying jobs and provide a stable income for their family.

3. **Mental Health Support:** Single motherhood can be a stressful and isolating experience, which can lead to mental health issues such as depression and anxiety. Providing mental health support services such as counseling, therapy, and support groups can help these mothers cope with the emotional challenges they face.

4. **Community Support:** Building a strong community support network for single mothers can provide them with a sense of belonging and social connection. This can include support groups, mentorship programs, and community events that cater to the needs of single mothers.

5. **Parenting Support:** Single mothers often have to navigate the challenges of parenting on their own, which can be overwhelming. Providing parenting classes, workshops, and resources can help these mothers develop the skills and knowledge needed to raise healthy and happy children.

6. **Access to Healthcare:** Many single mothers may not have access to affordable healthcare for themselves and their children. Providing access to healthcare services such as medical check-ups, vaccinations, and counseling can help improve their physical and mental health.

7. **Legal Support:** Single mothers may face legal challenges such as child custody disputes or child support issues. Providing legal support services such as free legal advice and assistance can help these mothers navigate the legal system and ensure that their rights are protected.

Supporting single mothers requires a comprehensive approach that addresses their financial, educational, mental health, social, parenting, health care, and legal needs. By providing support in these areas, we can help single mothers build a stable and secure future for themselves and their children.

Expanded family dynamics provide a way in which dedicated single mothers can be assisted while also adding to the value of the family they join.

Providing education and job training opportunities can be a key step in assisting single mothers to secure better-paying jobs and achieve financial stability. Here are some specific ways that education and job training can help:

1. **Enhancing Skills:** Education and job training programs can help single mothers develop new skills and improve existing ones, making them more competitive in the job market. This can include vocational training, certificate programs, and degree programs.
2. **Job Placement:** Some education and training programs have partnerships with employers and can provide job placement assistance to program graduates, helping them secure employment in their field of study.
3. **Flexibility:** Many single mothers face challenges balancing work and parenting responsibilities. Education and job training programs that offer flexible scheduling, online learning, and childcare options can make it easier for them to participate in and complete the program.
4. **Networking Opportunities:** Education and training programs can also provide networking opportunities, which can be valuable for single mothers who may not have a strong professional network. Connecting with professionals in their field can help them learn about job opportunities and build relationships that may lead to future job opportunities.
5. **Confidence:** Going back to school or pursuing job training can be a daunting experience, especially for those who may have been out of the workforce for some time. Education and training programs can help build confidence and provide support to single mothers as they

pursue their goals.

By providing education and job training opportunities to single mothers, we can help them develop the skills and knowledge needed to secure better-paying jobs and achieve financial stability for themselves and their families. This, in turn, can reduce the negative impacts of single motherhood, such as poverty and financial stress, and help build a stronger, more resilient community.

Large families can offer a strong community support network for single mothers. Being part of a large family can provide a sense of belonging and social connection, which is important for the mental health and well-being of single mothers and their children. Here are some specific ways that large families can support single mothers:

1. **Emotional Support:** Large families can provide emotional support to single mothers by offering a listening ear, a shoulder to cry on, and a sounding board for ideas and concerns. Family members can provide encouragement, validation, and reassurance during difficult times.
2. **Practical Help:** Large families can also provide practical help to single mothers by offering assistance with childcare, household chores, and errands. This can free up time and energy for single mothers to pursue work or education, or to simply take a break and care for themselves.
3. **Financial Support:** Large families can also provide financial support to single mothers by pooling resources and sharing expenses. For example, family members can chip in to pay for groceries, rent, or utilities, which can alleviate some of the financial burdens that single mothers face.
4. **Role Models:** Large families can provide positive role models for single mothers and their children. Seeing successful relationships and healthy communication within a family can help single mothers learn how to build healthy relationships and improve their communication

skills.

5. **Social Connections:** Large families can also provide social connections for single mothers and their children. Family gatherings, events, and traditions can provide opportunities for single mothers to connect with others, build friendships, and create new memories.

Being a member of a large family can be a valuable source of support and connection for single mothers. By providing emotional, practical, financial, and social support, large families can help single mothers navigate the challenges of single parenthood and build a strong foundation for themselves and their children.

Joining a loving family which is seeking to expand can be a viable option for single mothers who are seeking stability and support. However, it is important to approach this option with caution and to prioritize the safety and well-being of both the mother and her children. It is also essential to provide children with the support and resources they need to navigate this transition and develop a strong sense of identity and attachment.

Lastly, having a network of family members who can offer assistance and guidance can be incredibly valuable for single mothers. By building strong connections with their family and community, single mothers, with the assistance of the Divine Family Unit, can create a support system that can help them thrive and succeed in their personal and professional lives.

21

LEARNING HOW TO BE SUBMISSIVE AND NURTURING TO YOUR HUSBAND

The concept of Biblical submission in marriage is based on several key Biblical passages, including Ephesians 5:22-24 and Colossians 3:18-19, which instruct wives to submit to their husbands as to The Most High and to respect and love their husbands, respectively. The term "submission" in this context refers to willingly and respectfully yielding to your husband's leadership in the marriage, while also seeking to honor and please God.

It is important to note that submission in marriage is a mutual responsibility, with both spouses called to love and respect one another. However, the Bible specifically instructs wives to submit to their husbands as the head of the household, just as HaMashiach is the head of the church. This means acknowledging and respecting your husband's authority and leadership in the marriage, while also recognizing that he is called to sacrificially love and care for you, just as HaMashiach loved the church.

Many women today are curious about how they can be Biblically submissive wives to their husbands. They are extremely familiar with modern viewpoints but want to live a life in alignment with Biblical principles.

As a woman, and as a wife in this modern world, if you've been struggling with being submissive and supportive to your husband, this chapter will provide you with some best practices on how to be submissive according to Biblical principles.

Ephesians 5:33 instructs wives to show respect to their husbands, which means acknowledging their role as the head of the household and valuing their leadership in the marriage. However, it is important to note that respect is a two-way street in a healthy marriage, and husbands are also called to show love and respect to their wives.

Ultimately, both spouses should strive to honor and cherish one another in their marriage, as Ephesians 5:21 instructs, "submitting to one another out of reverence for HaMashiach."

Ephesians 5:22-24 instructs wives to submit to their husbands in the same way that the church submits to HaMashiach. This means willingly accepting your husband's leadership and guidance in the marriage, just as HaMashiach leads and guides the church. However, it is important to note that submission does not mean blindly following your husband's every command, especially if it goes against Biblical principles or involves sin.

As with any human relationship, there will be times when disagreements arise, and both spouses need to communicate openly and respectfully, seeking to understand and compromise with one another. Ultimately, the goal of submission is to honor God and build a strong, loving, and mutually respectful marriage.

Ephesians 5:25-28 instructs husbands to love their wives sacrificially, just as HaMashiach loved the church and gave himself up for her. As a wife, you should also love your husband and seek to build him up and support him in your marriage. This involves actively showing care, respect, and affection for your husband, as well as supporting his goals and aspirations. Just as husbands are called to love their wives as HaMashiach loved the church, wives are also called to love their husbands and seek to cultivate a loving and mutually respectful relationship.

In the areas of companionship and partnership, it is very important that a husband and wife work together and not only be in alignment with one another but also in alignment with The Most High's Divine Will.

Genesis 2:18 highlights the importance of companionship and partnership in marriage, with God creating Hawah, also known as Eve, as a "helper fit for" Adam. As a wife, you have a unique and valuable role as your husband's helper, supporting and assisting him in all aspects of your marriage. This includes emotional support, practical assistance, and spiritual encouragement, as well as sharing the joys and challenges of life.

It is important to recognize that being a helper does not diminish your value or worth as an individual, but rather reflects the beauty of a complementary partnership in marriage, with both spouses working together to honor God and build a strong, loving, and mutually supportive relationship.

When we apply the principles of companionship and partnership in the expansive family sense, we are multiplied in the goodness that arises when a man has multiple wives who share in his vision and pursuit of growing the family into a Divine Family Unit.

Philippians 2:3-4 encourages us to live in humility and to consider the needs and interests of others as more important than our own. In a marriage relationship, this means putting your husband's needs and desires above your own, seeking to serve him in humility and selflessness.

This includes being attentive to his needs, showing him respect, and actively looking for ways to support and encourage him. However, it is important to note that this does not mean neglecting your own needs or compromising your values and beliefs. Rather, it means seeking to find a healthy balance between caring for your well-being and seeking to serve your husband in love and humility. Ultimately, a successful marriage is built on mutual love, respect, and a willingness to serve one another.

Let's take a moment to look into some general information on how to be a Biblically submissive wife based on the teachings of the Bible.

First and foremost, it is important to understand that Biblical submission does not mean inferiority or weakness. Rather, it is a voluntary choice to respect and honor your husband's leadership in your marriage, just as HaMashiach submitted to the will of God the Father.

Here are some Biblical principles for being a submissive wife:

1. **Respect your husband** - Ephesians 5:33 states, "Let the wife see that she respects her husband." This means showing honor and deference to your husband's authority in your marriage.
2. **Submit to your husband** - Ephesians 5:22-24 says, "Wives, submit to your own husbands, as to the Lord. For the husband is the head of the wife even as HaMashiach is the head of the church... Now as the church submits to HaMashiach, so also wives should submit in everything to their husbands." This does not mean blindly following your husband's every command, but rather willingly accepting his leadership and guidance.
3. **Love your husband** - Ephesians 5:25-28 instructs husbands to love their wives as HaMashiach loved the church. As a wife, you should also love your husband and seek to build him up and support him in your marriage.

4. **Be a helper to your husband** - Genesis 2:18 says, "It is not good that the man should be alone; I will make him a helper fit for him." As a wife, you have a special role as your husband's helper, supporting and assisting him in all aspects of your marriage.

5. **Practice humility** - Philippians 2:3-4 teaches, "Do nothing from rivalry or conceit, but in humility count others more significant than yourselves. Let each of you look not only to his own interests but also to the interests of others." This means putting your husband's needs and desires above your own and seeking to serve him in humility and selflessness.

It is important to note that being a Biblically submissive wife does not mean tolerating abuse or mistreatment from your husband. If you are experiencing any form of abuse, it is important to seek help and support from a trusted source, such as a pastor, counselor, or domestic violence hotline.

One of the keys to being a Biblically submissive wife is to seek God's guidance and wisdom through prayer and studying the Bible. By following Biblical principles and seeking to honor God in your marriage, you can build a strong and loving relationship with your husband.

The ultimate goal of Biblical submission in marriage is to honor God by following His design for marriage and seeking to please Him in all things. This means recognizing that God has given specific roles and responsibilities to husbands and wives in marriage and seeking to fulfill those roles in a way that glorifies Him. By putting God first in your marriage and seeking to follow His principles of love, respect, and mutual submission, you can build a strong and lasting relationship that reflects His love and grace.

As Ephesians 5:22-24 instructs, wives are called to submit to their husbands as the head of the household, just as HaMashiach is the head of the church. This means recognizing your husband's authority and leadership in the marriage and being willing to follow his lead in making important decisions.

Again, it is important to note that this does not mean blindly following your husband's every command or decision. Rather, it involves respectfully communicating with your husband, expressing your thoughts and concerns, and seeking to find a mutually agreeable solution.

Ultimately, both spouses should be seeking to honor God and serve one another in love and humility, recognizing that their roles and responsibilities are part of God's design for marriage.

Open and respectful communication is a crucial aspect of a healthy and fulfilling marriage, and it is especially important when it comes to navigating differences of opinion or perspective. As Proverbs 15:1 states, "A soft answer turns away wrath, but a harsh word stirs up anger." This means that speaking to your husband gently and respectfully, even when you disagree with him, can help to prevent conflict and promote understanding.

It is also important to actively listen to your husband's perspective and seek to find a mutually agreeable solution, rather than insisting on your way. By approaching conflicts with humility, patience, and a willingness to work together, you can build a stronger and more harmonious marriage that honors God.

Humility is also a fundamental aspect of Biblical submission in marriage. This means recognizing that you are not always right and being willing to submit to your husband's leadership in a spirit of love and respect. As Philippians 2:3-4 states, "Do nothing from rivalry or conceit, but in humility count others more significant than yourselves. Let each of you look not only to his own interests but also to the interests of others." This involves setting aside your desires and seeking to serve your husband in love and humility, putting his needs before your own. By doing so, you can build a relationship that reflects HaMashiach's sacrificial love and grace, and honor

God in your marriage.

Do you pray for your husband? Prayer is an important part of being a Biblically submissive wife. It is important to pray for your husband's well-being, wisdom, and leadership in your marriage. As Proverbs 15:33 says, "The fear of YaHeWaHe is an instruction in wisdom, and humility comes before honor." Seeking God's wisdom and guidance through prayer can help you to submit to your husband's leadership and to support and encourage him in all aspects of your relationship.

This can involve actively looking for ways to help and serve him, expressing gratitude and appreciation for his efforts, and showing him respect and honor in your words and actions. By seeking to build him up and support him in all areas of your marriage, you can help to foster a strong and loving relationship that honors God.

Serving your husband in love and humility is an important aspect of being a Biblically submissive wife. This involves seeking to meet his needs and supporting his goals and aspirations, while also recognizing your own needs and boundaries.

As Colossians 3:23-24 says, "Whatever you do, work heartily, as for the Lord and not for men, knowing that from the Lord you will receive the inheritance as your reward. You are serving the Lord HaMashiach." This means that as you serve and support your husband, you are also serving and honoring HaMashiach.

However, it is also important to recognize that serving your husband does not mean sacrificing your well-being or compromising your values and boundaries. It is important to communicate your needs and boundaries to your husband respectfully and lovingly and to seek to find a mutually beneficial solution.

As 1 Corinthians 7:3-5 says, "The husband should give to his wife her conjugal rights, and likewise the wife to her husband. The wife does not have authority over her own body, but the husband does. Likewise, the husband does not have authority over his own body, but the wife does. Do not deprive one another, except perhaps by agreement for a limited time, that you may devote yourselves to prayer; but then come together again, so that Satan may not tempt you because of your lack of self-control."

This means that while you should seek to meet your husband's needs and desires, you should also communicate your own needs and boundaries respectfully and lovingly.

As a Biblically submissive wife, here is a recap of the key principles and best practices that you can follow to ensure you cultivate a lasting and fulfilling marriage with your husband, regardless of the family structure he seeks to establish:

1. **Seek to honor God in your marriage:** The ultimate goal of Biblical submission is to honor God in your marriage, by following His design for marriage and seeking to please Him in all things.
2. **Respect your husband's leadership:** Acknowledge and respect your husband's role as the head of the household, and be willing to follow his lead in making important decisions.
3. **Communicate openly and respectfully:** While you may have different opinions or perspectives on certain issues, it is important to communicate with your husband openly and respectfully, seeking to understand and compromise with one another.
4. **Cultivate a spirit of humility:** Humility is a key aspect of Biblical submission, as it involves recognizing that you are not always right and being willing to submit to your husband's leadership in a spirit of love and respect.
5. **Pray for your husband:** Pray for your husband's well-being, wisdom,

and leadership in your marriage, and seek to support and encourage him in all aspects of your relationship.

6. **Serve your husband in love:** Serve your husband in love and humility, seeking to meet his needs and support his goals and aspirations, while also recognizing your own needs and boundaries.

Biblical submission in marriage involves willingly and respectfully yielding to your husband's leadership, while also seeking to honor and please God in all aspects of your relationship. By following these principles, you can cultivate a strong and mutually supportive marriage that reflects God's love and design for marriage.

As a wife, one of your important roles is to nurture your husband, both emotionally and spiritually, in alignment with Biblical principles.

Additionally, you can show nurturing towards your husband by expressing your love and affection for him regularly. This can involve physical touch, such as hugging or holding hands, as well as verbal affirmations of your love and appreciation for him.

Another way to be nurturing towards your husband is to actively listen to him and show interest in his thoughts and feelings. Make an effort to understand his perspectives and engage in meaningful conversations with him. This can help to strengthen your emotional connection and foster a deeper level of intimacy in your relationship.

You can also nurture your husband by supporting his interests and hobbies. Encourage him to pursue his passions and find joy in the things he enjoys, and make an effort to participate in these activities with him when possible. This can help to build a stronger sense of partnership and camaraderie in your marriage.

Consider ways to serve your husband and help him in practical ways. This can involve anything from preparing his favorite meals to running errands for him or helping with household chores. By serving him in these small ways, you can demonstrate your love and commitment to him and show that you are invested in his well-being and happiness.

Physical touch is a powerful way to nurture your husband emotionally. It can help to create a deeper level of intimacy and connection in your marriage. This is just one aspect of nurturing your husband emotionally. It's important to also show him love and affection in other ways, such as through verbal affirmations, acts of service, and spending quality time together.

Active listening is a crucial component of nurturing your husband emotionally. It involves not only hearing what he says but also understanding his feelings and perspectives. When your husband speaks to you, make an effort to give him your undivided attention. Put down your phone, turn off the TV, and make eye contact to show him that you value his words.

As he speaks, try to understand his perspective by putting yourself in his shoes. Ask clarifying questions if necessary, and avoid interrupting or getting defensive. Respond with empathy and understanding, even if you don't necessarily agree with his point of view. This will help him feel heard and valued, which is an important part of emotional nurturing in a marriage.

By actively listening to your husband, you show him that you care about his thoughts and feelings and that you respect him as a person. This can help to deepen your emotional connection and strengthen your bond as a couple.

Encouraging words can be a powerful tool for nurturing your husband emotionally. Take the time to express your appreciation for the things he does for your family, and acknowledge his strengths and abilities. Let him know that you believe in him and support him, even when things are tough.

One way to do this is to make a habit of giving your husband specific compliments regularly. Instead of simply saying "thank you" when he does something helpful, try to be more specific. For example, you might say, "I appreciate the way you took care of the children today. You're such a patient and loving father." Or, "I'm so grateful for your hard work and dedication to providing for our family. You're an amazing provider and I feel so blessed to have you as my husband."

In addition to giving compliments, make an effort to encourage your husband when he's facing challenges or feeling discouraged. Be his biggest cheerleader, and remind him of his strengths and abilities when he's feeling down. Pray for him and offer words of encouragement, such as "I know you can do this. I believe in you."

By using your words to build up and encourage your husband, you can help to create a positive and nurturing environment in your marriage. This can deepen your emotional connection and strengthen your bond as a couple.

Taking an interest in your husband's hobbies and passions is also an excellent way to nurture him. By showing genuine interest in what he likes, you are demonstrating your love and support for him as a person, not just as a husband.

Serving your husband in practical ways is another way to be nurturing toward him. Serving your husband can be a way of expressing your love for him. You can consider his likes and dislikes and cater to them in small ways to show him that you are thinking of him. This could be as simple as making his favorite breakfast or packing him a lunch for work. Additionally, you can take care of his needs by washing his clothes, ironing his shirts, or running errands for him.

By serving your husband in practical ways, you show him that you are committed to making his life easier and more enjoyable, and this can go a long way in nurturing your relationship. It is important to note that serving your husband should not be done out of obligation or as a way to manipulate him, but rather as a genuine expression of love and care.

Lastly, nurturing your husband's spiritual growth is an important aspect of being a Biblically nurturing wife.

Now we will recap and review some of the ways to incorporate physical touch into your relationship, as well as how you can help your husband grow in his faith. Remember to nurture your husband, both emotionally and spiritually, in alignment with Biblical principles, and you will see your marriage grow to the heights you've always prayed and hoped for:

1. **Pray for him:** One of the most nurturing things you can do for your husband is to pray for him regularly. Pray for his well-being, wisdom, and spiritual growth, and ask God to guide him in his leadership of your marriage and family. Encourage him to pray as well.
2. **Show affection:** Physical touch, such as holding hands, hugging, or kissing, can be a powerful way to nurture your husband emotionally. Make an effort to show affection towards him regularly, and let him know that he is loved and valued.
3. **Listen actively:** Take the time to listen actively to your husband when he speaks to you. This means giving him your full attention, making eye contact, and responding with empathy and understanding.
4. **Speak words of affirmation:** Use your words to build up and encourage your husband. Tell him how much you appreciate him and the things he does for your family, and affirm his strengths and abilities.
5. **Support his interests:** Take an interest in your husband's hobbies and passions, and encourage him to pursue them. Attend his events or activities, and show him that you value and support his interests.
6. **Serve him:** Look for ways to serve your husband in practical ways,

such as cooking his favorite meal or doing a chore he dislikes. This shows him that you care about his well-being and are willing to go out of your way to make him happy.

7. **Encourage his spiritual growth:** Help your husband grow in his faith by reading the Bible together, praying together, or attending church together. Encourage him to seek God's guidance in all aspects of his life.

8. **Hold hands:** Holding hands is a simple gesture that can be incredibly comforting and reassuring. It can help to strengthen your emotional connection and create a sense of closeness between you and your husband.

9. **Hug often:** Hugging is another powerful way to show affection and nurture your husband. It can help to reduce stress and increase feelings of happiness and well-being. Make an effort to hug your husband regularly, especially when he is feeling down or stressed.

10. **Give a kiss:** A kiss is a simple yet powerful way to show your husband that you love him. Make an effort to kiss him goodbye in the morning and hello when he comes home from work. You can also surprise him with a kiss during the day just to show him that you are thinking of him.

11. **Cuddle up:** Spending time cuddling with your husband can be incredibly comforting and relaxing. It can help to reduce stress and create a sense of emotional closeness. Make an effort to cuddle up with your husband on the couch or in bed, and enjoy the warmth and comfort of each other's company.

12. **Ask him about his interests:** Take the time to learn more about your husband's hobbies and passions. Ask him questions, and show a genuine interest in what he has to say. This will help you to better understand him and his interests.

13. **Attend his events:** Whether it's a concert, a sports game, or a hobby-related event, make an effort to attend with him. Even if you're not particularly interested in the activity, being there with him will show your support and love.

14. **Help him pursue his interests:** Encourage your husband to pursue his interests by providing him with the time and resources he needs. If he needs a specific tool or equipment for his hobby, consider gifting it to him or helping him find it.

15. **Share in his experiences:** If your husband is passionate about something, chances are he loves to talk about it. Listen actively, and ask questions to show you're engaged. Also, try to share in the experiences with him. For example, if he loves hiking, plan a weekend getaway to a national park and take in the beautiful scenery together.

16. **Be open-minded:** Even if your husband's interests aren't something you would normally enjoy, be open-minded and try to see the appeal in them. This will help you to connect with him on a deeper level and show him that you respect and appreciate him for who he is.

- Read the Bible together and discuss what you have learned. You can choose a Bible study or devotional book to guide your discussions.

- Attend church together regularly, and participate in church activities such as small group Bible studies or volunteer work.

- Encourage your husband to seek out fellowship with other Israelite men, such as through a men's Bible study or accountability group.

- Support your husband in his spiritual practices, such as prayer, meditation, or reading Scriptural books.

- Share your faith journey with your husband, and be open to learning from him as well.

- Serve others together as a couple, through volunteering at your church or in your community.

When you commit to nurturing your husband's spiritual growth, you are not only helping him deepen his relationship with God but also strengthening your marriage by building a strong foundation on shared values and beliefs.

Remember, nurturing your husband is not about being subservient or sacrificing your own needs and boundaries. It is about loving and supporting him in a way that honors God and strengthens your marriage.

As 1 Peter 3:7 says, "Husbands, live with your wives in an understanding way, showing honor to the woman as the weaker vessel, since they are heirs with you of the grace of life, so that your prayers may not be hindered." By nurturing your husband, you are helping to create a strong and fulfilling marriage that honors God.

Your expanding family depends upon your ability to adapt. Be present, and be intentional in assisting your husband in being the best version of himself daily. When he wins, you win, and the entire family wins. Keeping this in mind will help you solidify your "why". Your "why" is the deeper reason you commit to a goal without wavering.

There will be times when you feel isolated because expanded families are still not seen as the norm in today's modern society. However, maintaining your prayer life and keeping a level head through all adversity will surely positively benefit you.

Cultivating open dialogue with your husband about your feelings and emotions will allow you both to gauge your growth and appreciate the small successes you achieve together.

22

CREATING ECONOMIC OPPORTUNITIES FOR YOUR EXPANDING FAMILY

As families grow and expand, there may come a time when you want to consider creating economic opportunities for your family members. This could involve starting a family business, creating employment opportunities within an existing business, or exploring other ways to provide financial support to your loved ones. While creating economic opportunities for your expanding family can be a noble goal, it is important to approach it responsibly and sustainably.

Additional Streams Of Revenue

Expanding your family can certainly present the need for additional streams of revenue, and starting a family business can be a great way to achieve this goal. By considering each family member's skills and talents, you can create a business that is tailored to the strengths of the family as a whole.

When starting a family business, it's important to keep in mind that it may not be feasible or desirable to employ every member of the family. Some family members may have interests or skills that don't align with the business, or they may have other career aspirations that don't involve working in the family business. It's important to have open and honest communication with your family members about their goals and interests and to make sure that the decision to employ them in the family business is based on their skills and qualifications rather than simply because they are family.

If you do decide to employ family members in the family business, it's important to establish clear expectations and boundaries from the beginning. This means setting up formal employment agreements that outline job responsibilities, compensation, and any other relevant details. It's also important to treat family members like any other employee and to avoid playing favorites or showing preferential treatment.

In addition to starting a family business, there are other ways to establish multiple streams of revenue for your family. For example, some families may choose to invest in rental properties or stocks, while others may start side businesses or pursue freelance work. The key is to explore a variety of options and find what works best for your family's unique situation and goals.

Expanding your family can present the need for additional streams of revenue, and starting a family business can be a great way to achieve this goal. By considering each family member's skills and talents, and by setting clear expectations and boundaries, you can create a successful and sustainable business that supports your family's financial goals. Additionally, there are other ways to establish multiple streams of revenue, and it's important to explore a variety of options and find what works best for your family.

Consider the Skills and Interests of Your Family Members

When considering creating economic opportunities for your family members, it is important to think about their skills and interests. You want to ensure that the work they do is something they enjoy and are good at, which will lead to greater job satisfaction and ultimately, greater success. For example, if you are considering starting a family business, you may want to think about what skills and expertise each family member can bring to the table. If someone is particularly skilled in marketing, they may be well-suited to handle advertising and promotions for the business.

Maintain Professionalism and Avoid Nepotism

One potential challenge when creating economic opportunities for your expanding family is the risk of nepotism. Nepotism occurs when someone in a position of power favors family members over other employees, regardless of their qualifications or abilities. This can lead to resentment and a toxic work environment. It is important to maintain professionalism and treat family members like any other employee. This means setting clear expectations, holding them to the same standards as everyone else, and offering constructive feedback when needed.

Ensure Fair Compensation

When employing family members, it is important to ensure that they are being fairly compensated for their work. This means paying them market rates and not taking advantage of the fact that they are family. It can be helpful to set up a formal employment agreement outlining job responsibilities, compensation, and any other relevant details. This will help ensure that everyone is on the same page and there are no misunderstandings or hard feelings down the road.

Consider the Long-Term Sustainability of Your Business

While employing family members can be a great way to keep the business in the family and create a lasting legacy, it is important to consider the long-term sustainability of the business. This means ensuring that the business is profitable and has a solid plan for growth and succession. It is also important to have a plan in place for what will happen if a family member decides to pursue other opportunities or if there are conflicts within the family that make it difficult to work together.

Be Responsible, Be Sustainable

Creating economic opportunities for your expanding family can be a great way to build a lasting legacy and keep the business in the family. However, it is important to approach it responsibly and sustainably. This means considering the skills and interests of your family members, maintaining professionalism, ensuring fair compensation, and considering the long-term sustainability of the business. By following these guidelines, you can create a successful and fulfilling business that supports both your family and your goals.

As mentioned earlier in this chapter, creating economic opportunities for your expanding family can be a noble goal, but it is important to do so responsibly and sustainably. Here are some things to consider:

1. **Consider the skills and interests of your family members:** When looking to provide employment opportunities for your family members, it is important to consider their skills and interests. You want to ensure that they are doing work that they enjoy and are good at, which will ultimately lead to greater success and job satisfaction.

2. **Maintain professionalism and avoid nepotism:** It is important to maintain professionalism and avoid nepotism when employing family members. This means treating them like any other employee and holding them to the same standards as everyone else.

3. **Ensure fair compensation:** It is important to ensure that your family members are being fairly compensated for their work. This means paying them market rates and not taking advantage of the fact that they are family.

4. **Consider the long-term sustainability of your business:** While employing family members can be a great way to keep the business in the family and create a lasting legacy, it is important to consider the long-term sustainability of the business. This means ensuring that the business is profitable and has a solid plan for growth and succession.

Overall, creating economic opportunities for your expanding family can be a great way to build a lasting legacy and keep the business in the family. However, it is important to do so while considering the skills and interests of your family members, maintaining professionalism, ensuring fair compensation, and considering the long-term sustainability of the business.

While creating economic opportunities for your expanding family can certainly help keep them within the family dynamic and build a lasting legacy, it is important to remember that there may be other factors at play when it comes to your family members' employment opportunities. For example, some family members may have different career aspirations or interests that may not align with the business you are building.

it's important to keep in mind that not all family members may have the same career aspirations or interests that align with the business you are building when creating economic opportunities for your expanding family. While it can be tempting to assume that all family members will want to be a part of the family business, it's important to consider that they may have their own goals and aspirations.

It's also important to have open and honest communication with your family members about their career aspirations and interests. This means creating an environment where family members feel comfortable discussing their goals and aspirations without feeling pressured to conform to the family business. By understanding their interests and goals, you may be able to find creative ways to incorporate their skills and expertise into the family business or identify other opportunities that align with their career aspirations.

You will also have to keep an open mind when it comes to supporting family members who may choose to pursue other career opportunities outside of the family business. This means encouraging and supporting their growth and development, even if it means they won't be a part of the family business. By supporting them in their pursuits, you can build a strong and supportive family dynamic that celebrates each family member's unique talents and aspirations.

Remember to have open and honest communication with your family members about their goals and aspirations, and to support them in pursuing their path if that is what they choose. Additionally, it is important to consider the economic realities of your business and whether it can realistically support employment for all family members.

In summary, while creating economic opportunities for your expanding family can be a worthwhile goal, it's important to remember that not all family members may be interested in participating in the family business.

By maintaining open and honest communication and supporting each family member's aspirations, you can build a strong and supportive family dynamic that celebrates each member's unique talents and goals.

23

MAINTAINING RESPECT AND DIGNITY IN YOUR FAMILY AS THE MAN

Give Respect To Get Respect

Growing up throughout boyhood, we often hear the phrase "To get respect, you have to give respect." Once we reach manhood, this phrase has oftentimes been drilled into our thought process and it becomes second nature for us. From an action-based perspective, as well as from an expectation-based perspective, many men have this idea of giving respect to get respect instilled in them as a main pillar of life.

Raising a family is no small task. In the area of expanded family, the task only gets larger. As the man in your family, you are called upon daily because you have positioned yourself to be the leader and guide for multiple people. To effectively lead your Divine Family Unit, you must establish respect and dignity for yourself early on.

Establishing respect doesn't mean that you have to be a dictator, where everyone does everything you command them to do at all times. Cultivating your dignity doesn't mean that you have to belittle others to make yourself feel superior either. Instead, you have to focus on your self-worth daily and move in a way where each member of your family is inspired and motivated to do their absolute best in life because they see you doing your absolute best in life.

Communication is one of the most important factors in maintaining respect and dignity in any relationship, including within a family. When we communicate effectively, we create a space for open dialogue, understanding, and mutual respect.

Active listening is an essential component of effective communication. It means giving your full attention to the speaker, without interrupting or being judgmental. When we actively listen, we show empathy and understanding, which can help to foster respect and trust.

Expressing ourselves clearly and respectfully is also crucial. We should strive to communicate in a way that is easy for everyone to understand and that avoids hurtful or derogatory language. Instead, we should focus on building each other up by offering encouragement, support, and positive feedback.

What To Do When Conflict Arises

When conflicts arise, it's important to approach them with a calm and respectful attitude. Avoid attacking or blaming the other person, and instead, focus on finding a solution that works for everyone. By working together to overcome challenges, we can build stronger relationships and maintain mutual respect and dignity within our families.

Taking the time to establish clear boundaries and expectations for acceptable behavior is essential in maintaining respect and dignity within a family too. It is important to communicate openly and honestly with each other to ensure that everyone understands what is and isn't acceptable behavior.

One way to do this is by setting family rules or guidelines that everyone can agree on. These rules could include things like treating each other with respect, using positive language, and avoiding derogatory or hurtful comments. By establishing clear guidelines, everyone will know what is expected of them and what behaviors are unacceptable.

It's also important to hold everyone accountable for their actions. If someone violates the family rules, they should be held responsible for their behavior. This doesn't mean that punishment is always necessary, but it does mean that the person should acknowledge their mistake and work to make amends.

Encouraging open communication is another key component of maintaining respect and dignity within a family. Everyone should feel comfortable speaking up when they feel disrespected or when there is a conflict. Encourage your family members to express their feelings and opinions peacefully and respectfully.

When conflicts do arise, it's important to work together to find a resolution that is respectful and fair to everyone involved. This could involve compromise, active listening, and a willingness to see things from the other person's perspective. By working together to find a solution, everyone can feel valued and respected, even in challenging situations.

Overall, establishing clear boundaries, holding everyone accountable for their actions, and encouraging open communication and conflict resolution are crucial in maintaining respect and dignity within a family. By working together, families can create a positive and supportive environment that promotes the well-being and happiness of all members.

Maintaining respect and dignity in your family as a man is an essential aspect of being a good partner, father, and role model. It is important to create an environment where everyone feels valued, heard, and respected. Here are some ways to maintain respect and dignity in your family:

1. **Communicate effectively:** Communication is key to maintaining respect and dignity in any relationship. Make sure you listen to what your family members have to say and express yourself clearly and respectfully. Avoid using hurtful or derogatory language, and instead, focus on building each other up. Listen to each other with an open mind, and express yourself respectfully. Communicate in a way that is easy for everyone to understand and make sure to address any misunderstandings or conflicts promptly.

2. **Practice active listening:** Active listening means paying attention to what the speaker is saying, without interrupting or being judgmental. When someone is speaking to you, give them your full attention. Show that you are interested in what they have to say by making eye contact, asking questions, and offering feedback. It's also important to show empathy and understanding by putting yourself in their shoes. When you listen actively, you create a space for respectful dialogue and understanding.

3. **Establish clear boundaries:** Every family has its unique set of rules and boundaries, so it is important to establish clear guidelines on what behavior is and isn't acceptable. These boundaries should be communicated to everyone in the family, and there should be consequences for violating them. Consistency is key when enforcing boundaries.

4. **Encourage positive interactions:** Encourage your family members

196

to treat each other with kindness and respect. Celebrate each other's accomplishments, and work together to overcome challenges. It's important to model good behavior by treating everyone in the family with kindness and respect.

5. **Show appreciation:** Let your family members know that you value and appreciate them. Take the time to acknowledge their accomplishments and express gratitude for the contributions they make to your family. Small gestures, such as saying thank you, can go a long way in fostering mutual respect and appreciation.

6. **Address conflicts promptly:** Conflicts are inevitable in any family, but it's important to address them in a respectful and timely manner. Avoid sweeping problems under the rug or letting them escalate. Encourage everyone to voice their concerns, and work together to find a solution that works for everyone.

7. **Lead by example:** As the man of the family, you have the opportunity to set the tone for how your family interacts with each other. Be a positive role model by treating others with kindness and respect, and encouraging your family members to do the same.

8. **Create a culture of respect:** Establish clear boundaries for what is and isn't acceptable behavior in your family, and hold everyone accountable for their actions. Encourage your family to speak up when they feel disrespected and work together to resolve conflicts peacefully and respectfully.

9. **Foster trust:** Trust is an essential ingredient in any healthy relationship. Be open and honest with your family members, and encourage them to do the same. Avoid betraying their trust by keeping your promises and being reliable.

10. **Be supportive:** Your family members should always know that you have their back. Whether it's helping with homework, listening to a problem, or simply offering words of encouragement, be there for your family members when they need you.

Showing Mutual Appreciation

Creating a culture of mutual appreciation and support is key to maintaining respect and dignity in your family as a man. By leading by example, communicating effectively, setting clear boundaries, and fostering trust, you can help ensure that your family members feel valued, heard, and respected.

Maintaining respect and dignity in your family also requires consistent effort and communication. By establishing clear boundaries, encouraging positive interactions, and addressing conflicts promptly, you can create a home environment where everyone feels like their opinions and viewpoints matter. This will instill within them the feeling of being valued and respected. Remember to practice active listening, show appreciation, and model good behavior to create a happy and healthy family dynamic.

As the man of the family, you have a unique role in setting the tone for how your family interacts with each other. You can be a positive role model by treating others with kindness and respect and encouraging your family members to do the same. Here is a list of suggestions and best practices to help you get the ball rolling in the right direction:

1. **Use positive language:** Avoid using negative language or making critical comments. Instead, focus on using positive language to build others up and show your support.
2. **Show empathy:** Try to put yourself in other people's shoes and understand their perspectives. Show that you care by offering support and encouragement when someone is going through a tough time.
3. **Apologize when necessary:** If you make a mistake or hurt someone's feelings, take responsibility for your actions and apologize. This shows that you value and respect the other person's feelings.
4. **Set clear expectations:** Establish clear boundaries and expectations

for how family members should treat each other. Make sure everyone understands what is and isn't acceptable behavior, and follow through with consequences when necessary.

5. **Be a role model:** Model the kind of behavior you want to see in your family. Treat others with kindness and respect, and encourage your family members to do the same. Show that you value and respect everyone's contributions to the family. You should also show your family members how to support each other by being intentional in your support of their endeavors. Demonstrate kindness, empathy, and support in your actions and words.

Remember that as the man of the family, you have a powerful influence on how your family interacts with each other, so take the opportunity to be a positive role model and promote a culture of kindness and respect.

Establishing Trust

As you are expanding your family, you will soon find out, if you haven't already, that trust is a critical component of maintaining respect and dignity within a family. Without trust, it can be difficult to build strong and healthy relationships with our loved ones.

1. **Be open and honest:** Honesty is the foundation of trust. Be transparent with your family members and avoid hiding things from them.
2. **Keep your promises:** If you make a promise to your family member, make sure you follow through. Breaking promises can erode trust over time.
3. **Be reliable:** Make sure your family members can count on you. Show

up when you say you will, and be there for them when they need you.

4. **Avoid betraying their trust:** If a family member confides in you, keep their confidence. Avoid sharing their personal information or betraying their trust in any way.

5. **Communicate openly:** Encourage your family members to communicate openly with you. Let them know that you value their opinions and are willing to listen.

6. **Apologize and make amends:** If you make a mistake or hurt someone's feelings, be willing to apologize and make things right. This can help rebuild trust and strengthen your relationship.

Being Open And Honest

By being open and honest with your family members, keeping your promises, and avoiding betraying their trust, you can create a strong foundation of trust within your family. This can help promote mutual respect and dignity and foster healthy and supportive relationships with your loved ones.

When we take the time to acknowledge the contributions and accomplishments of our loved ones, it can strengthen our relationships and foster a sense of mutual respect and appreciation.

Here are some ways to express gratitude and appreciation towards your family members:

1. **Acknowledge their accomplishments:** When someone in your family achieves something significant, take the time to acknowledge

their hard work and celebrate their success.

2. **Show your appreciation for their contributions:** Whether it's cooking dinner, doing the laundry, or helping with homework, make sure your family members know that you appreciate their efforts and contributions to the family.

3. **Say "thank you" often:** A simple "thank you" can go a long way in showing your family members that you value and appreciate them.

4. **Give compliments:** Take the time to give compliments and positive feedback to your family members. Let them know that you notice and appreciate their positive qualities and traits.

5. **Spend quality time together:** Spending time together as a family is a powerful way to show your appreciation and strengthen your relationships. Make time for family outings, dinners, and activities that everyone can enjoy.

By expressing gratitude and appreciation towards your family members, you can create a positive and supportive family environment that promotes mutual respect and dignity. Remember to take the time to acknowledge and celebrate the contributions and accomplishments of your loved ones, and let them know how much you value and appreciate them.

Supporting The Members Of Your Family

Supporting your family members is an essential part of maintaining respect and dignity within your family. When we support our loved ones, we show them that they are valued and cared for, and this can strengthen our relationships with them. Here are some ways to support your family members:

1. **Be there for them:** When a family member needs help or support, be there for them. This can involve helping with homework, listening to their problems, or just spending time with them.

2. **Offer words of encouragement:** When a family member is going through a difficult time, offer words of encouragement and support. Let them know that you believe in them and that they can get through it.

3. **Celebrate their successes:** When a family member achieves something significant, celebrate their success and let them know that you are proud of them.

4. **Respect their choices:** Even if you don't always agree with your family member's choices, it's important to respect them. This can help promote mutual respect and dignity within your family.

5. **Learn from our mistakes:** Teach your family that we all make mistakes. Being available for your family members when they make mistakes is incredibly powerful. When we illustrate the importance of learning from our mistakes and letdowns, we inspire a resilient and tenacious attitude within each member of our Divine Family Unit.

6. **Be open about your own mistakes:** Share your own mistakes with your family members and let them know what you learned from them. This can help create a safe space for everyone to talk about their mistakes and learn from each other.

7. **Focus on learning, not failure:** When a family member makes a mistake, focus on what they can learn from it rather than on the mistake itself. This can help promote a growth mindset and encourage them to try again.

8. **Encourage problem-solving:** Instead of solving problems for your family members, encourage them to come up with their solutions. This can help promote critical thinking and problem-solving skills.

9. **Celebrate progress:** When a family member learns from their mistakes and makes progress, celebrate their achievements and let them know that you are proud of them.

10. **Practice forgiveness:** It's important to forgive each other for mistakes

and move forward. Holding grudges or dwelling on mistakes can create unnecessary tension and conflict within the family.

Making Mistakes

It's important to teach our family members that making mistakes is a natural part of life and that we can learn from our experiences. This can help promote a growth mindset and resilience within our family, which can ultimately lead to greater respect and dignity for each other.

By teaching our family members about the importance of learning from mistakes, we can help promote a growth mindset, as well as resilience. This can ultimately lead to greater respect and dignity within your family as everyone learns to support each other through their challenges and setbacks.

It's not ok to be toxic in the way we think or to continue perpetuating toxic behaviors, just because "that's what we experienced and got through, so our families can too." Cussing at, and belittling our family members when they make mistakes is never a good thing to do. Many of us weren't raised within the type of loving and supportive family environment that we are seeking to build and establish for our family today. It's ok to make mistakes along the way and to question if what you are doing is correct. Take a moment to pray and reflect on how you want to guide your family. Then make the necessary adjustments needed to manifest your thoughts into your reality.

By fully committing to supporting your family members, you can create a strong and supportive family environment that promotes respect and dignity. Remember to be there for your loved ones when they need you, offer words of encouragement, and celebrate their successes.

Establishing and maintaining your dignity and respect has everything to do with being of service to your family, and being intentional in the positive ways you treat them. Start with the man in the mirror, and become the change that you'd like to see reflected within your Divine Family Unit.

You will get your respect, and you will have your dignity because those are the attributes and qualities you are extending to your family members daily.

24

HOW TO RECOGNIZE IF YOUR WIFE IS DEPRESSED OR FEELING LEFT OUT

When Your Wife Feels Left Out

I n this modern society, the topic of polygyny is not an easy one to converse about. There are multiple television shows available today which have been produced in an attempt to oppose the Biblical narrative, as well as the instructions given by The Most High about expanded family. These shows make it easy for today's modern women to stand against the Divine union of polygyny, in favor of other forms of polygamy that are not ordained by The Highest. Many modern women will seek to align themselves with the popular viewpoints of today, and will oftentimes feel isolated or threatened by the ancestral approaches to marriage brought forth from within The Scriptures.

When the subject of expanding your family arises, you may receive some pushback from your initial, or first wife. One of her defensive reasoning tactics will be based solely on what she has seen and learned from the polygamy-based television programming that Hollywood is actively promoting. She will be quick to reference these shows filled with toxicity and immorality, and will likely refuse to listen to the sound doctrine and reasoning involving expanded family, as presented to us within the Scriptures.

If your wife does take a moment to listen to the Biblical narrative about polygyny, she will dismiss it as a practice long forgotten, which is no longer relevant to today's ever-evolving lifestyles. Very rarely will your wife be open to hearing your perspective on expanding your family in a non-judgmental way, so maintain respect towards her willingness to be open-minded by conducting your due diligence on the subject before bringing it to her in conversation.

One aspect of this process which you will have to expect is that even when your wife agrees to listen to you and honor your request to have the difficult conversations about expanding your family, she will question if supporting you and your decision to expand your family was the correct one. The likelihood of her facing a bout of depression is extremely high in the beginning phases of expanding your family.

Having a societal spotlight placed on her will not be easy to cope with early on, and she will feel ostracized for her decision to participate in polygyny. You must be thorough in your explanations to her regarding your vision and be willing to extend prodigious amounts of patience to her as she accepts the direction you are leading your family.

The majority of the people on earth, both men and women, have a herd mentality. However, most women seek an illusionary level of comfort when they stay within the confines of societal norms and expectations. Feeling left out, or soloed out from their peer groups and social circles, is not something that most women find appealing or acceptable.

This is why you, as your wife's husband, must become an even greater confidant and friend to your wife once you decide to expand your family. Assuming that she will think and feel the same as you about expanding your family would be foolish. You will have to come to grips that for the most part, women do not want to share their husbands. The conversations that you have with your wife should not be based on manipulation and coercion, but should instead be based on facts and truth.

Emphasis must be placed on the types of marriages that The Most High has ordained. Our Hebraic culture is a direct antithesis to the modern acceptable standard of marriage and relationships. You and your wife should desire to live within the tenets and principles established for us in The Scriptures.

If one, or both of you, is new to the truth about the vast perspective on the Biblical Family structure, it is highly recommended that you take the time to familiarize yourselves with the varied narratives contained within The Scriptures. This book is one resource that seeks to assist you in moving in the right direction by highlighting these Scriptural narratives in a concise and easy-to-read format.

When your wife feels left out of peer groups and social circles, it's important to cultivate an environment for her where she can identify her uniqueness and flourish within her creative pursuits. Becoming productive and receiving the appreciation that comes with a job well done for creating something new and unique will make her feel valued and deserving of her newly found success.

As men and husbands, it's important to factor in the necessity of supporting our wives in finding their sense of identity and purpose. Encourage her to pursue her interests and passions, and provide her with opportunities to develop her skills and talents.

One way to do this is by helping her identify her strengths and providing her with resources and support to cultivate those strengths. Encourage her to explore new hobbies and activities, and help her connect with others who share her interests. Her original social circles will change during your expanded family's growth. The adage is true: "Birds of a feather flock together". However, we must utilize great wisdom when facilitating new affiliations and social groups that align with the principles we've established for our family.

Allowing your wife to continue being around naysaying women who will only scoff at her decisions to support you will not be good for either of you, so you want to emphasize the quality of her associates over the number of her associates. One of the best people to introduce your first wife to should eventually be your subsequent wife.

Make this arrangement a personal goal of yours by slowly acclimating them to each other. You don't want to force this relationship on either of them, especially if they didn't know one another previously to your marriages to both of them. However, you do want to consistently drive the importance home to both of them that you have a goal for the entire family to be harmonious and work together on one accord, so becoming cordial and being respectful of one another is a necessity.

You can also help create a supportive and positive environment at home by showing appreciation for your wife's efforts and accomplishments. Celebrate her successes, no matter how small they may seem, and encourage her to continue pursuing her goals.

Remember that everyone has unique strengths and talents, and it's important to support and celebrate those differences. By helping your wife cultivate her sense of identity and purpose, you can help her feel valued and appreciated, which can have a positive impact on her emotional well-being and overall happiness.

Feelings Of Depression Are To Be Expected

It's important to approach your wife with empathy and openness if you suspect that she may be feeling depressed or left out in your marriage.

You can start by asking her how she's feeling and letting her know that you're there to listen. Avoid interrupting or dismissing her feelings or perspective, and try to be patient and understanding as she shares her thoughts and concerns.

Validating your wife's feelings and letting her know that you take them seriously is extremely important and will show her that you are emotionally supportive and not selfish. Let her know that you care about her and want to support her, and ask her what you can do to help.

If your wife is open to it, you can also suggest seeking professional help, such as therapy or counseling, from a sister who is actively involved in an expanded family dynamic. Remember, it's okay to not have all the answers, and seeking professional assistance can be a helpful and supportive step toward healing and improving your marriage.

If your wife is depressed or feeling left out in your marital decisions, you should take a moment to look at everything from her perspective. This doesn't mean that your perspective isn't valid, or that you won't be able to move forward with your plans about marrying another woman. What it does mean is you are taking the time to address her valid concerns about expanding your family in a loving manner which will indicate to her that you truly care about her emotional state and want her to be comfortable with the final decision you make as the husband and leader of your family.

It's important to approach any marital decision, including the decision to engage in polygyny, with sensitivity and respect for your wife's feelings and concerns. If your wife is feeling left out or depressed, it's especially important to take the time to listen to her perspective and understand how the decision may impact her emotionally.

It's just as important to create a safe and supportive space where your wife can express her concerns without fear of judgment or criticism. Try to be patient and understanding as she shares her thoughts and concerns, and avoid interrupting or dismissing her feelings.

You can also take steps to reassure your wife that you value and care for her. Let her know that you are considering her feelings and concerns in your decision-making process, and be open to discussing ways to address any issues that arise.

When it comes to reassurance, reassuring your first wife is just as important as reassuring your second wife. Both of these women love you, and it's important to realize that they will both have concerns about your marriage to them, but from slightly different perspectives.

Your first wife will initially feel as though you no longer love her, and are trying to replace her. Your subsequent, or incoming wife, will feel as though she doesn't hold as much value in your life because you've been married to your first wife for a longer period, so any small marital infraction on her part, as an incoming wife, will cause you to want to put her away. Both women will need reassurance and confirmation from you as their husband, that they hold a special place in your life and that both of them are valued members within your expanded family dynamic.

Reassuring both wives can be a daunting task. Making them feel valued and appreciated in your family dynamic is one aspect of polygyny that many men expect to naturally happen. This is one area of your expanded family that you must be intentional about being consistent in. Each wife may have different concerns and perspectives, but it's important to listen to their individual needs and concerns and address them in a loving and supportive manner.

Keep in mind that reassuring your first wife is particularly important, as she may feel like her place in the family is being threatened or that she is being replaced. It's important to assure her that your love and commitment to her have not diminished and that you value her as a spouse, partner, and member of your Divine Family Unit.

At the same time, it's equally important to acknowledge the concerns and feelings of your incoming wife and make her feel welcome and valued in your expanded family dynamic. Help her to understand that you are committed to building a strong and loving relationship with her and that you will work together to create a happy and harmonious family.

It's also important to communicate openly and honestly with both wives and to be transparent about your feelings and intentions. Building trust and mutual understanding is key to creating a healthy and successful polygynous relationship. A successful polygynous relationship requires mutual respect, communication, and a commitment to creating a loving and supportive family dynamic for all members involved. This is easier said than done, so you must be committed to your family, as well as to your vision.

Proverbs 16:1-3 tells us that the preparations of the heart belong to man, but the answer of the tongue is from **YaHeWaHe**. The passage goes on to remind us that all the ways of a man are pure in his own eyes, but **YaHeWaHe** weighs the spirits. Lastly, we are advised to commit our works to **YaHeWaHe**, and our thoughts will be established.

Ultimately, any decision regarding polygyny should be made with the input and consent of all parties involved. If your wife is not comfortable with the idea, it may be necessary to explore other options or find ways to address her concerns. Remember that a healthy and loving marriage involves mutual respect, communication, and understanding and that your wife's emotional well-being should be a top priority.

If you suspect that your wife may be feeling depressed, left out in your marriage, or ostracized in her social circles, it is important to take her feelings seriously and seek to address the issue. Here are some signs to look out for:

1. **Loss of interest in activities:** If your wife used to enjoy certain hobbies or social activities, but now seems disinterested or withdrawn from them, it may be a sign of depression.
2. **Changes in sleeping and eating habits:** Depression can affect a person's appetite and sleep patterns. If your wife is eating more or less than usual, or has trouble sleeping or sleeps excessively, it may be a sign of depression.
3. **Emotional changes:** Your wife may become more irritable, sad, or anxious than usual. She may also seem more sensitive to criticism or rejection.
4. **Lack of energy:** Depression can make even simple tasks feel overwhelming. Your wife may seem more tired or lethargic than usual and may have trouble completing basic household tasks.
5. **Withdrawal from intimacy:** If your wife seems distant or disinterested in physical intimacy, it may be a sign of emotional distress.
6. **Expressing feelings of loneliness or isolation:** Your wife may express feelings of loneliness or isolation, even if you spend a lot of time together.

A loss of interest or withdrawal from previously enjoyed hobbies and social activities can be a sign of depression. It's important to be aware of any changes in your wife's behavior or mood and to take notice if she seems disinterested or unengaged.

Depression is a serious mental health condition that can have a profound impact on a person's quality of life, and it's important to seek professional help if you suspect your wife may be struggling with it. Encourage your wife to speak with a mental health professional who can provide her with the support and resources she needs to manage her symptoms and improve her overall well-being.

In addition to seeking professional help, there are several things you can do to support your wife and help her manage her depression. Encourage her to stay engaged in activities she enjoys, even if she doesn't feel like it at first. Offer to participate in these activities with her, or help her find new hobbies or social activities that may interest her.

You can also help create a supportive and positive environment at home by showing empathy, understanding, and patience. Avoid placing blame or judgment on your wife, and instead focus on providing her with the emotional support and encouragement she needs to overcome her depression.

Changes in appetite and sleep patterns can be common symptoms of depression as well. Your wife may experience a loss of appetite and lose weight, or she may eat more than usual and gain weight. Similarly, she may have trouble sleeping, experience insomnia, or sleep excessively.

It's important to pay attention to any changes in your wife's eating or sleeping habits and to encourage her to seek professional help if you suspect she may be struggling with depression.

In addition to seeking professional help, there are several things you can do to support your wife and help her manage her depression. Encourage her to establish a regular sleep schedule and to practice good sleep hygiene, such as avoiding caffeine and electronics before bedtime.

You can also encourage her to eat a healthy and balanced diet and to engage in regular physical activity. Exercise has been shown to have a positive effect on mood and can help alleviate symptoms of depression. It's important to approach the situation with empathy and understanding and to avoid placing blame or judgment on your wife for her symptoms.

Changes in mood and emotional state are also recognized as common symptoms of depression. Your wife may feel more irritable, sad, or anxious than usual, and may seem more sensitive to criticism or rejection.

Again, it's important to be aware of any changes in your wife's mood or emotional state and to approach the situation with empathy and understanding. Encourage her to seek professional help if you suspect she may be struggling with depression, as a mental health professional can provide her with an accurate diagnosis and develop a personalized treatment plan to help manage her symptoms.

In addition to seeking professional help, there are several things you can do to support your wife and help her manage her depression. Encourage her to practice self-care and to engage in activities that promote relaxation and stress relief, such as yoga, meditation, or deep breathing exercises.

You can also help create a supportive and positive environment at home by showing extreme patience and the willingness to grow through the emotional fluctuations with your wife. Avoid placing blame or judgment on your wife, and instead focus on providing her with the emotional support and encouragement she needs to overcome her depression. Establishing an expanded family is not for the mentally weak or the faint of heart.

Depression can even cause physical and mental fatigue, making everyday simple tasks feel overwhelming. Your wife may seem more tired or lethargic than usual and may struggle with completing basic household tasks. Offer to help her with various household tasks and responsibilities, and encourage her to take breaks and practice self-care when needed.

Changes in physical intimacy can also be a sign that your wife is experiencing emotional distress. If your wife seems distant or disinterested in physical intimacy, it's important to approach the situation with wisdom and sound judgment.

Encourage your wife to communicate openly about her feelings and emotions, and try to identify any underlying issues that may be affecting your physical relationship. Make sure that you work together to find solutions that work for both of you.

Physical intimacy is an important aspect of a healthy marriage, but it's also important to prioritize emotional intimacy and communication. By working together to address any underlying emotional issues, you can strengthen your relationship and improve your overall emotional well-being.

Hopefully, you've realized by now that your wife can express feelings of loneliness or isolation, even if you spend a lot of time together. However, spending a lot of time together doesn't mean that the time spent is quality time. Make an effort to spend quality time with your wife, engage in activities that you both enjoy and show appreciation for her contributions to your life and your relationship.

The entire family's emotional well-being is of the utmost importance. When your wife is emotionally stable, the household will operate a lot smoother. Emotional well-being as an important aspect of a healthy marriage, is a necessity that must be established and tended to throughout your expanded family dynamic. By working together to address any underlying issues, you can strengthen your relationship and improve your family's emotional health all across the board.

Remember that depression is a treatable condition, and with the right support and resources, your wife can regain her joy, passion, and emotional well-being, and improve her overall quality of life. If you notice any of these signs, it's important to approach your wife with empathy and understanding. Encourage her to seek professional help if needed, and work together to address any underlying issues in your marriage.

The Energy Shift Into Negativity

When your wife negatively changes her energy towards you, your marriage becomes increasingly draining and frustrating, which can sometimes cause you as the husband, to want to retreat from the relationship instead of confronting the underlying issues that make her feel that overwhelming sense of negativity.

If you decide that expanding your family is the best decision, you need to realize early on that it's understandable how when your wife negatively changes her energy toward you, your marriage can become draining and frustrating. However, retreating from the relationship is not the best course of action, as it can lead to further disconnection and may worsen the situation.

Instead, it's important to confront the underlying issues that are causing your wife to feel negative and to work together to address them. This may involve having open and honest communication about how you both feel and actively listening to each other's concerns.

As men, we don't like to address the overly emotional aspects of a relationship, but when you expand your family into a Divine Family Unit, you will also have to expand your thinking and overall thought process regarding the women in your life. If you get frustrated easily and do not exercise patience consistently, you may want to reconsider taking on such a huge responsibility until you work those aspects of your personality out in a positive manner.

Confronting underlying issues in a marriage can be a sensitive and difficult process, and the difficulty only multiplies with the more wives you marry, but it's important for the health and longevity of the relationships you are establishing and seeking to cultivate. Here are some steps and best practices that can help you confront the underlying issues and work together with your wife or wives to address them:

1. **Start with open and honest communication:** Sit down with your wife in a calm and comfortable environment, and express your concerns and feelings about the negative changes in your marriage. Encourage her to share her feelings and concerns, and actively listen to what she has to say without judgment or interruption.

2. **Identify the underlying issues:** Together, try to identify the specific issues that are causing your wife to feel negative. This may involve discussing past events or behaviors that have caused tension or hurt or identifying current stressors that are impacting your relationship.

3. **Seek outside help if necessary:** If you're having trouble identifying or addressing the underlying issues, it may be helpful to seek the assistance of a therapist or counselor. A professional can provide you both with objective guidance and support and help you work through any emotional or communication barriers.

4. **Develop an improvement plan:** Once you've identified the underlying issues, work together to develop an improvement plan. This may involve setting specific goals, establishing boundaries and guidelines for behavior, or seeking outside resources such as books or workshops on communication and relationships.

5. **Follow through and be patient:** Addressing underlying issues in a

marriage takes time, patience, and commitment from both partners. Be willing to follow through on your plan for improvement, and be patient as you work through any challenges or setbacks along the way.

Focus on finding solutions together and working towards healthier and happier marriages. A strong and healthy marriage requires effort and commitment from both partners and by working together, you can overcome the challenges and build a stronger and more fulfilling relationship.

People handle emotions and stressful situations differently. When confronting the emotional instability of your wife, or wives, you want to do your absolute best to create methods of assistance that are customized for each of them. What you do for one, may not be advised for what you do when it comes to your assistance towards the other.

Women can feel when you aren't being genuine towards them too, so you want to take a moment to stand back and reflect on the best way to go about handling a situation as complex as emotional instability. Dealing with emotions comes with the turf of expanding your family and there is no way to ignore this fact.

Keep your focus and do your best not to absorb the emotional reactions of your wife. Instead, be emotionally stable, patient, and recognize that you are her head, and should be able to guide her in righteousness to the sort of solutions that will benefit her, yourself, and the entire Divine Family Unit.

25

IGNORING WHAT SOCIETY HAS TO SAY ABOUT YOUR MARRIAGE DECISIONS

D eciding to expand your family is not an easy one at all. In this day and age, you will have to contend with so many differing viewpoints, doubts, and concerns. Most of these viewpoints, doubts, and concerns will come from people who are not vested fully in your life. However, these people will always seem to have a superior influence in our lives as long as we pay attention to them instead of paying attention to our pursuits and happiness.

One of the major issues expanded families face is gossip and allowing people in their business. People love to gossip about what others are doing, or not doing, mainly because it allows them to divert the attention away from themselves, which would otherwise be used to condemn them in pertinence to something they are or are not doing.

You will have to learn to get used to the spotlight and have a microscope on you if you are going to expand your family. If you were never popular or aren't used to having a ton of attention on you, get ready, because you will have all sorts of attention once you finalize your decision. Your wives will more than likely be ostracized, and you will be judged for your vision and leadership abilities.

Gossip and interference from others can incite major issues for polygynous families. Here are a few tips and best practices that may help you and your family deal with these issues:

1. **Establish boundaries:** It's important to establish clear boundaries with family, friends, and community members from the beginning. Make it clear what topics are off-limits for discussion, and communicate your expectations for privacy and respect. This can help prevent others from meddling in your family's affairs.

2. **Be selective with whom you share information:** Not everyone needs to know the intimate details of your family's life. Be selective with whom you share information, and only share what you feel comfortable with. This can help prevent gossip and rumors from spreading.

3. **Focus on your happiness:** When you're living a lifestyle like polygyny, which is non-traditional in a Western societal context, it's important to focus on your happiness and well-being. Don't let the opinions of others bring you down, and remember that your and your family's happiness is what matters most.

4. **Surround yourselves with supportive people:** Surrounding yourself with supportive people can make a huge difference in how you cope with gossip and interference. Seek out friends and family members who are accepting of your lifestyle and can offer you emotional support when you need it. It's important to have a strong support system when you're living an expanded family lifestyle. Seek out friends and family members who support your decision and can offer encouragement and guidance when you need it. You may also want to seek out other polygynous couples or communities where you can connect with

others who share your lifestyle.

5. **Educate others:** Sometimes, gossip and interference can come from a place of ignorance or misunderstanding. By educating others about your lifestyle and why it works for your family, you may be able to dispel some of the myths and misconceptions surrounding polygyny. One way to combat negative opinions and judgments is to help others learn about polygyny and why it works for you and your husband. By sharing your experiences and explaining your decision, you may be able to change some people's minds and help them understand your lifestyle better.

Establishing clear boundaries with family, friends, and community members is important for any family, but it's especially crucial for polygynous families. By setting clear boundaries from the beginning, you can help prevent others from meddling in your family's affairs and avoid any potential misunderstandings or conflicts.

Some examples of boundaries you may want to establish include:

- **Privacy:** Let others know that your family's personal life is off-limits for discussion. You may want to specify that you won't be sharing details about your family's intimate relationships or finances, for example.

- **Respect:** Communicate your expectations for how you and your family members should be treated. Let others know that you won't tolerate any disrespect or judgmental comments about your lifestyle.

- **Topics of discussion:** Make it clear what topics are off-limits for discussion. This can include anything from your family's religious beliefs to your personal opinions on politics or social issues.

- **Visits and communication:** Set expectations for how often you'll see or communicate with family and friends. Let others know that you appreciate their interest in your family, but you also value your privacy and alone time.

It's crucial that you, as the husband, set the tone and communicate your boundaries clearly and assertively, but also respectfully. Let others know that you're open to discussion and questions, but that you also expect them to respect your wishes. By establishing clear boundaries and sticking to them, you can help protect your family's privacy and maintain healthy relationships with others.

Your wives will also feel more secure and protected in moving forward with you as you decide the best route to take in regards to growing your expanded family if you establish the early precautionary measures needed to ensure that boundaries are in place for those who might want to intrude in your marriages.

We all have family, friends, and associates that we want to impress. Being selective with whom you share information can be an effective way to prevent gossip and rumors from spreading. While it's natural to want to share important news or updates with friends and family members, it's important to consider who you're sharing this information with and whether they're likely to respect your privacy.

Some tips for being selective with whom you share information include;

- **Stick to the facts:** When sharing information about your family, stick to the facts and avoid embellishing or sharing personal opinions. This can help prevent misunderstandings and minimize the risk of gossip.

- **Consider the person's track record:** If you have a friend or family member who has a history of spreading rumors or gossiping, it's best to avoid sharing sensitive information with them.

- **Use discretion on social media:** Be mindful of what you share on social media and who can see it. Consider adjusting your privacy settings or using a more private platform to share updates about your family.

- **Be aware of the context:** When sharing information with others, be aware of the context and whether it's appropriate to share personal details. For example, sharing intimate details about your family at a public gathering may not be appropriate.

Selectively choosing whom you share information with can also help protect your family's privacy and prevent gossip and rumors from spreading. It's important to use discretion and consider the context when sharing personal details about your family with others.

Another important point that must be drilled home is that when you are conversing with your wives "on the one", meaning having an exclusive conversation with them separately, and at different times, you don't want to be the cause of tension between them by sharing intimate details from a conversation that one wife had with you, with your other wife.

Respect the integrity of the relationships you are cultivating with both of your wives by not sharing what you talk about with one, to the other. You will build trust within your Divine Family Unit and will also provide the space for your wives to converse with one another about the topics that they share with you in confidence when the time arrives for them to do so.

Living a non-traditional lifestyle (according to Roman Westernized standards) like polygyny can come with its own unique set of challenges and judgments from others. However, it's important to remember that ultimately, your happiness and well-being, as well as the happiness and well-being of your family, is what matters most.

Here are some more tips and best practices for focusing on your happiness and well-being:

- **Surround yourself with supportive people:** Seek out friends and family members who are accepting of your lifestyle and who will support you and your family. This can help you feel more confident in your choices and can provide a valuable source of emotional support.

- **Prioritize self-care:** Make time for self-care activities that help you feel relaxed and rejuvenated. This could include things like exercise, meditation, or hobbies that you enjoy.

- **Stay true to your values:** Focus on your values and priorities, and don't let the opinions of others sway you from your path. Remember that you and your family are the ones who ultimately have to live with your decisions, so it's important to stay true to yourselves.

- **Find community:** Seek out others who are living a similar lifestyle, either in person or online. This can provide a sense of community and belonging and can help you feel less isolated in your choices.

The overall goal here is to prioritize your happiness and well-being and not let the opinions of others bring you down. Focus on what matters most to you and your family, and don't be afraid to seek out support and community along the way.

There is an adage that says "When the student is ready, the teacher will appear." There is a newer adage that goes something like this: "When you purchase a motor vehicle, you begin to see that same type of vehicle all over the place, when you previously had never noticed it." Ok, I might've just made that one up, but the truth of the matter is that we attract what we have deep interests in. Likewise, we will begin to attract other Divine Family Units to our circle once we accept the truth and reality of our decision to establish and cultivate our expanded family.

This brings us to our next point: having a supportive network of friends and family members can be a valuable resource for anyone, especially those living in an expanded family dynamic. When facing gossip and interference from others, having people who accept and understand your lifestyle can make a huge difference in how you cope and navigate those challenges.

Here are some tips for building a supportive network:

- **Seek out like-minded individuals:** Look for local or online groups for people who share your lifestyle or beliefs. These groups can be a great place to connect with others who understand your experiences and can offer advice and support.

- **Be open and honest:** When talking to friends and family members about your lifestyle, be open and honest about your experiences and feelings. This can help them understand your perspective and can open the door for deeper conversations and support.

- **Look for non-judgmental listeners:** Sometimes, you may just need someone to listen without judgment or unsolicited advice. Look for friends or family members who are good listeners and who can offer a safe space for you to talk about your experiences.

- **Consider therapy:** If you're struggling with the challenges of polygyny, therapy can be a great resource for working through those challenges and building a support network.

Building a supportive network is well worth it, and can help you cope with the challenges of living in an expanded family dynamic like polygyny. By seeking out like-minded individuals, being open and honest, looking for non-judgmental listeners, and considering therapy, you can find the support you need to thrive.

Most men won't opt to participate in therapy, so another way you can get the assistance you need is by attending business seminars that focus on team management or connecting with a mentor whose opinions and advice you can trust.

Educating others about your lifestyle and why it works for your family can be a powerful way to dispel myths and misconceptions surrounding polygyny, and can help others understand and accept your lifestyle.

Here are some tips for educating others about polygyny:

- **Be prepared:** Before starting a conversation about polygyny, make sure you have a good understanding of what it is and how it works. This can help you answer questions and address concerns clearly and confidently.

- **Start with the basics:** When talking to someone who may be unfamiliar with polygyny, start with the basics. Explain what it is, how it works, and why it works for your family.

- **Share your experiences:** Share your own experiences with polygyny and how it has impacted your life and relationships. This can help others see the benefits of polygyny and understand why it works for your family.

- **Address common misconceptions:** Many people may have misconceptions about polygyny based on stereotypes or misinformation. Address these misconceptions directly and provide accurate information to help dispel them.

- **Be respectful and patient:** Remember that not everyone will immediately accept or understand your lifestyle. Be patient and respectful, and try to approach conversations with an open mind and a willingness to listen.

Educating others about polygyny can be a powerful way to dispel myths and misconceptions and help others understand and accept your lifestyle. By being prepared, starting with the basics, sharing your experiences, addressing common misconceptions, and being respectful and patient, you can help others see the benefits of polygyny and why it works for your family.

You might even inspire others to consider expanding their family dynamic, so when you do have that conversation with them, it's important to deliver the facts, and just as important that you are comfortable in your stance and views of yourself.

Dealing with gossip and interference can be challenging, even for the most seasoned polygynous families. However, by establishing clear boundaries, being selective with whom you share information, focusing on your happiness, surrounding yourselves with supportive people, and educating others, you can minimize the impact of these issues and live a happy, fulfilling life.

Ignoring The Pressures Of Society When It Comes To Our Marital Decisions

When you, as the husband, choose for your family to live a polygynous lifestyle, one of your hopes should be that your initial wife supports your decision. It is extremely difficult to confidently move forward with any decisions we make in life as men when the people closest to us do not support us in the direction we seek to move towards. When our wives are included in that number of non-supportive individuals, it can hurt deeply.

The issue is that society has its judgments about your decisions, which can affect how your wife views your actions and vision. Learning to ignore these societal judgments will be of great benefit to you in the long run, but how do you focus on yourselves and tune out the naysayers and haters?

Ignoring societal pressures can help us stay focused on what we truly want and need in our marriage, which can help us stay committed to our goals and aspirations. By doing so, we can build a strong and fulfilling relationship with our spouse based on our values and beliefs, rather than conforming to societal expectations. It allows us to prioritize our happiness and well-being in our marriage, rather than trying to meet the expectations of others.

It can be challenging to tune out societal judgments and criticisms, especially when it comes to an expanded family lifestyle choice like polygyny. However, there are a couple of things you and your husband can do to focus on yourselves and tune out the naysayers and haters:

1. **Focus on your happiness:** At the end of the day, what matters most is that you and your husband are happy with your decision to live in a polygynous relationship. Remember why you made this decision in the first place, and focus on building a happy, fulfilling life together.

By prioritizing your happiness, you can tune out the negative opinions of others and feel more confident in your decision.

2. **Tune out negativity:** It can be tempting to engage with naysayers and haters, but it's usually not worth your time or energy. Instead, focus on tuning out negativity and surrounding yourself with positivity. Avoid reading negative comments or engaging with people who are openly hostile or judgmental. Remember that their opinions are not a reflection of you or your lifestyle.

It's important to remember that you and your husband made the decision to live in a polygynous relationship because it works for you both, and that's what matters most. By prioritizing your happiness and focusing on building a fulfilling life together, you can tune out the negative opinions of others and feel more confident in your decision.

It can be challenging to live an expanded family lifestyle, but by staying true to yourselves and your goals as a family, you can overcome these challenges and build a happy, healthy life together. Remember to communicate openly and honestly with each other, establish clear boundaries with others, and seek out supportive friends and family members who can offer you emotional support when you need it.

At the end of the day, the most important thing is that you and your husband are happy and fulfilled in your relationship. By focusing on your happiness and well-being, you can create a life together that is fulfilling, rewarding, and full of love.

Having a strong support system can make a huge difference in how you cope with the challenges that come with living in an expanded family lifestyle. Seeking out friends and family members who are accepting and supportive of your decision can provide you with a much-needed sense of belonging and validation.

Additionally, connecting with other polygynous couples or communities can be an excellent way to find support and guidance. It can be helpful to connect with others who have gone through similar experiences and can offer advice and encouragement based on their own experiences. You may also be able to find resources and information on how to navigate the unique challenges that come with polygynous relationships.

Remember that it's okay to seek out support and guidance when you need it. Living in an expanded family lifestyle can be challenging at times, and having a strong support system can make all the difference in how you cope with those challenges.

Educating others can be a powerful tool in combatting negative opinions and judgments about polygyny. Sharing your experiences and explaining why this lifestyle works for you and your husband can help others understand that polygyny is a valid and fulfilling choice for some families.

It's important to approach these conversations with patience and understanding, as some people may be resistant to accepting something that is outside of their own cultural or social norms. However, by sharing your story and providing information, you may be able to change some people's perspectives and reduce the stigma surrounding polygynous relationships.

Keep in mind that not everyone will be open to understanding or accepting your lifestyle, and that's okay. You don't have to convince everyone to approve of your choices. What matters most is that you and your husband are happy and fulfilled in your relationship.

You will have to learn how to embrace the importance of prioritizing your own mental and emotional well-being and avoid engaging with negativity as much as possible. It's natural to feel defensive or hurt when faced with criticism or judgment, but responding with anger or defensiveness will likely only escalate the situation.

Instead, focus on surrounding yourself with positivity and support. Seek out communities of like-minded individuals who understand and accept your lifestyle, and spend time with friends and family members who are supportive of your decision.

It's also important to set boundaries with people who are consistently negative or judgmental towards you and your relationship. This may mean limiting your interactions with them or even cutting them out of your life entirely if they are toxic or harmful.

Remember that you have the power to control how you react to negative opinions and judgment. By focusing on your happiness and well-being, and surrounding yourself with positivity and support, you can tune out the negativity and live a fulfilling life in your polygynous relationship.

Overall, it's important to remember that your decision to live in a polygynous relationship is a personal choice that works for you and your husband. By focusing on your happiness, surrounding yourselves with supportive people, educating others, and tuning out negativity, you can stay true to yourselves and live the life you want, regardless of societal judgments.

Ignoring The Pressures Of Society When It Comes To Your Husband

Ignoring societal pressures can help you, as a wife, stay focused on what you truly want and need in your marriage to your husband in several ways.

Firstly, societal pressures can create a lot of noise and confusion in your decision-making process, making it difficult for you to identify and prioritize your wants and needs. By ignoring these pressures, you can more easily identify and focus on what is truly important to you and your relationship with your husband.

Secondly, societal pressures can create unrealistic expectations and standards for what a marriage should be like, which can cause you to compare your marriage to others and feel inadequate or dissatisfied. By ignoring these pressures, you can create a more authentic and personalized marriage that works for you and your husband, rather than trying to conform to societal expectations.

Thirdly, turning a blind eye to societal pressures can help you build a stronger and more genuine connection with your husband. When you prioritize your own needs and wants in your marriage, you are more likely to communicate openly and honestly with your husband, which can help you build trust, intimacy, and mutual understanding in your relationship.

Overall, ignoring societal pressures can help you stay focused on your wants and needs in your marriage to your husband, which can lead to a stronger, more authentic, and fulfilling relationship.

Ignoring The Pressures Of Society When It Comes To Your Wife

Ignoring the external pressures and expectations of this modern society can help us stay focused on what we truly want and need in our marriage to our wives. As men, we have to learn how to fortify ourselves against the haters and naysayers. We also have to conduct ourselves in a way where we can deflect what others have to negatively say, and be mentally strong enough to stand on the decisions we make. Here are some helpful ways on how we can do this:

1. **Reducing external influences:** Societal pressures can sometimes create unnecessary external influences on our marriage decisions, causing us to feel pressured to conform to societal expectations. By ignoring these pressures, we can focus on what truly matters to us and our wives, and make decisions based on our values and beliefs.

2. **Improved communication:** Ignoring societal pressures allows us to focus on the unique dynamics of our relationship with our wife, and can encourage more open and honest communication. By prioritizing our wants and needs, we can communicate more effectively with our wives and work together to build a stronger and more fulfilling marriage.

3. **Strengthening intimacy:** By ignoring societal pressures and focusing on our own needs and wants, we can create a more intimate and meaningful connection with our wives. This can help us build a deeper understanding and appreciation for one another, and create a more fulfilling and satisfying marriage.

4. **Building a stronger foundation:** By ignoring societal pressures and focusing on what truly matters to us and our wives, we can build a stronger foundation for our marriage. This foundation is built on mutual respect, trust, and a deep understanding of one another's needs and wants, which can help us weather any challenges that may arise in our marriage.

The societal pressures we experience daily can be overwhelming and can lead us to make decisions that are not aligned with our desires and values. Ignoring these pressures can help us stay true to ourselves and our spouses, and make decisions that are best for our marriage and family. It can also allow us to be more authentic and genuine in our relationships, which can ultimately lead to greater happiness and fulfillment.

When we can tune out societal pressures, we can focus on building a strong relationship with our wife and work towards our shared goals and aspirations. By prioritizing our wants and needs, we can communicate more openly and honestly with our wives, which can lead to a deeper connection and greater understanding. This can help us build a marriage that is unique to us and tailored to our specific needs and desires, rather than conforming to external expectations.

As we prioritize our own needs and desires, we can better communicate with our wives and build a deeper connection based on mutual understanding and respect. This can lead to a more fulfilling and satisfying marriage, where both partners feel heard, valued, and supported. Additionally, by ignoring societal pressures, we can break free from outdated and restrictive norms, and create a marriage that is uniquely tailored to our values and beliefs.

By prioritizing our own needs and wants, we can build a stronger and more authentic connection with our wife or wives, which in turn can strengthen the foundation of our marriage or marriages. This can also help us approach challenges and conflicts more productively, as we are better able to communicate and work together towards solutions that work for all of us. Ultimately, building a strong foundation based on mutual respect and understanding can lead to a more fulfilling and long-lasting marital arrangement.

Establishing and cultivating an expanded family is more nuanced than many would like to believe. Due to the nature of not being an acceptable form of marriage in Western society, a large number of well-established expanded families keep to themselves, not sharing the do's and don'ts that are learned and adhered to along the journey to Divine Family Unit fulfillment.

The silver lining to all of this is that the ongoing force of societal pressures can help us create a more authentic, fulfilling, and satisfying marriage with our wife or wives. It allows us to prioritize our own needs and wants, communicate more effectively, strengthen intimacy, and build a stronger foundation for our relationships.

Judgmental Friends?

It's truly unfortunate when our friends become overly judgmental about our marital choices and decisions. There could be a variety of reasons why they are behaving this way, but it's important to remember that their behavior is not a reflection of you or your choices.

One possibility is that your friends may have their ideas and expectations about what a successful marriage looks like, and they may be projecting those expectations onto you. They may not understand or respect your vision for your marriage and may be trying to influence your decisions based on their own beliefs and values. The majority of the people who will project their beliefs and values onto you will either not be married themselves or they will be living within a miserable marriage reflecting their envy and jealousy onto you.

Be prepared for people who claim to be close to you, watching your every move from the outside looking in. Some of them will be brave enough to ask you about your intentions while in a polygynous arrangement, however, the taboo topic of polygyny will cause them to be crass and make the questions they ask you uncomfortable to answer.

Do your best to answer their questions patiently and with love, no matter how difficult the questions seem to be. Treat each uncomfortable interaction as a practice session in building your character and fine-tuning your patience. You will learn to welcome these sorts of uncomfortable questioning sessions once you realize that they will eventually become comfortable enough for you to deal with. You will know that you've grown emotionally when you begin to answer people's questions with a level of surety and confidence that, ironically, makes them uncomfortable.

Another possibility is that your friends may be struggling with their insecurities or fears about marriage, and may be using your situation as a way to validate their own choices or beliefs. They may be judging you to make themselves feel better or more secure about their own decisions.

Watching you establish and grow your Divine Family Unit can also inspire feelings of resentment and hatred towards you because you are exhibiting a level of courage not often seen in this modern age, and because you are living the type of life you desire to live. You are also living the type of life that your friends secretly desire to live, but don't dare to establish for themselves. Effectively communicating with your wives and confidently leading your family is going to be paramount in your success moving forward.

Regardless of the reason for their behavior, it's important to remember that you have the right to make your own choices and decisions about your marriage. You are the one who knows your own needs, wants, and aspirations, and your friends should respect and support your vision for your own life.

If their behavior continues to be a problem, it may be helpful to have an open and honest conversation with them about how their judgment is affecting them. You could try explaining your perspective and asking them to respect your choices and decisions, or you may need to consider distancing yourself from those friends who cannot support and respect your vision for your own life.

Making decisions about our personal lives, including our marriage decisions, is a highly personal and individual choice. While it is important to consider the opinions of your loved ones, ultimately, the decision should be based on what is best for you and your spouse.

To do better for ourselves and the legacy we hope to leave behind, we need to learn to ignore societal pressures and expectations when it comes to marriage decisions. This means being aware of the societal norms and beliefs surrounding marriage, but not allowing them to dictate our choices. We can do this by:

1. **Understanding our values and beliefs:** Before making any decisions, we need to understand our values and beliefs when it comes to marriage. This means examining our personal goals, priorities, and aspirations, and understanding what we want from a partner and a marriage.
2. **Being open-minded:** While it is important to have a clear idea of what we want, we also need to be open-minded and willing to consider different perspectives and possibilities. Being open-minded can help us make better decisions and lead to more fulfilling relationships.
3. **Trusting ourselves:** Ultimately, we need to trust ourselves and our instincts when it comes to marriage decisions. We know ourselves better than anyone else, and we need to have confidence in our ability to make the right choice for ourselves.

Understanding our values and beliefs is an important step in making any decision, especially when it comes to marriage. By reflecting on our personal goals and aspirations, we can better understand what we want from a partner and a marriage, and make more informed decisions that align with our values and beliefs. This can help us build a stronger and more fulfilling relationship with our partner, based on shared values and a common vision for the future.

Being open-minded is crucial in any relationship. It allows us to approach situations with a willingness to learn and grow, rather than getting stuck in our ways. When we are open-minded, we can consider different perspectives, challenge our own biases, and explore new possibilities that we may have never considered before. This can lead to more meaningful and fulfilling relationships with our loved ones.

Trusting ourselves and our instincts is crucial when it comes to making any kind of decision, especially one as important as choosing a life partner. We should take the time to reflect on our values, needs, and aspirations, but ultimately, we should trust our gut and make the decision that feels right for us. By doing so, we can build a strong and fulfilling relationship with our spouse.

By maintaining our emotional composure throughout the varied societal pressures and expectations, we can make better decisions for ourselves and the legacy we hope to leave behind. We can create relationships and marriages that are based on our values and beliefs, rather than what society tells us we should do.

Courting A Woman

Courting a woman can be a fun and advantageous process for both parties to get to know one another and to figure out if a relationship is viable between the two.

Courting a woman can also be a great way to build a strong foundation for a relationship. It allows both parties to get to know each other respectfully and intentionally and can help establish a deeper connection and understanding.

During the courting process, it's important to be respectful, attentive, and communicative. Show genuine interest in her life and interests, and listen actively when she speaks. Be open and honest about your thoughts and feelings, and don't be afraid to ask questions or share your own stories.

It's also important to be patient and take things slow. Rushing into a relationship can lead to misunderstandings and disappointment, so allow the relationship to develop naturally over time. This can also help build trust and a stronger emotional connection.

Taking the time to court a woman can be a rewarding and fulfilling experience, as long as it's done with respect, communication, and an open mind.

Courting a woman involves getting to know her, building a connection, and establishing a Hebraic relationship. Here is some advice on how to court a woman:

1. **Show genuine interest:** Show interest in the woman's life, hobbies, and passions. Listen to her when she talks and ask questions to get to know her better.
2. **Be a gentleman:** Be respectful, courteous, and chivalrous. Open doors for her, offer to pay for meals and be kind and considerate in your words and actions.
3. **Communicate clearly:** Be open and honest in your communication. Express your intentions clearly and listen to her feelings and thoughts as well.
4. **Spend quality time together:** Plan dates and activities that you both enjoy. This can help you build a connection and create memorable experiences together.
5. **Build emotional intimacy:** Share your thoughts, feelings, and aspirations. This can help you build a deeper connection and establish trust.
6. **Be patient:** Remember that building a strong connection takes time. Don't rush into things, but instead allow your relationship to develop naturally.
7. **Respect boundaries:** Be mindful of the woman's boundaries and respect them. Don't pressure her into anything she's not comfortable

with.

Genuinely showing interest in a woman's life and passions is an important aspect of courting. This can help build a connection and show that you value her as a person beyond just physical attraction. It's important to listen actively and ask thoughtful questions to show that you are genuinely interested in getting to know her better.

Being respectful, courteous, and chivalrous is important when courting a woman. It shows that you value and appreciate her, and it can make her feel special and cared for. Additionally, it can set a positive tone for the relationship and lay the groundwork for mutual respect and kindness.

You need to be comfortable with transparency in your communication and actions. Open and honest communication is crucial in any relationship, especially during the courting phase. Being clear about your intentions and expectations can help avoid misunderstandings and ensure that both parties are on the same page. It's also important to actively listen to the woman and take her thoughts and feelings into consideration. Effective communication is the foundation of a healthy relationship.

Let her know that you intend to meet her parents eventually, especially her father, to share with them how you view life and marriage. This way she will be more comfortable with you knowing that you aren't trying to sneak and creep around with your vision for an expanded family.

If you can have a constructive sit-down, ideally with her father, she will see that you are serious and that you aren't afraid to confront differing societal viewpoints, especially if her father and mother should oppose your decision. If you are hesitant to participate in this crucial step, you should probably reconsider building an expanded family until you are comfortable with yourself enough to confidently express your vision to others when required.

Planning dates and activities that both you and the woman enjoy can be a great way to bond and get to know each other better. You can suggest doing activities like hiking, cooking, attending concerts or shows, or exploring a new city together. It's important to consider the woman's interests and preferences as well and be open to trying new things. This can also show that you value her input and care about her enjoyment of the relationship.

Sharing your thoughts, feelings, and aspirations is important in building a deeper connection and establishing trust. It's essential, to be honest and transparent with each other to ensure that you're both on the same page about what you want from the relationship. Being vulnerable and sharing personal information can also help to create intimacy and build emotional bonds between you and the woman you're courting.

Another great point that should be shared is that building a strong connection does take time and it's important not to rush things. It's important to let the relationship develop naturally and not force anything. Rushing into things can create unnecessary pressure and can potentially harm the relationship. Taking things slowly can help build a stronger and more meaningful connection.

Make sure that you inform her from the outset of the courting process that you are seeking to expand your family, and that you are interested in polygyny. Do not string her along or make her feel as though she will be the only woman in your life. If she can accept your decision to grow an expanded family great, and if she doesn't, kindly let her know that you think it would be best if you went your separate ways because your goals don't align with one another.

If she is the perfect match for you, and you eventually get married to this woman, you will then take the steps required to make her feel special in your alone time with each other. She will come to cherish and appreciate this alone time more, while also enjoying her role as a valued member of the Divine Family Unit. You must be intentional throughout this aspect of your marriage though.

She can be the finest, most beautiful woman you ever laid eyes on, but if her viewpoints and life goals don't align with yours, it's important to identify this early on, and not force your views onto her. This is the point in the courting process where you have to keep it real and stand on what you envision for yourself and your family. Don't waste time hoping that this woman changes her mind or immediately decides to rock with you in growing your family.

It's crucial that you give thanks to The Highest for revealing the truth of the situation to you, and that you pray to The Most High on her behalf that she is led to the man that suits her best, and that He guides you to the woman that will suit you best.

Lastly, respecting the woman's boundaries is crucial in any relationship. It's important to establish clear boundaries from the beginning and communicate openly about them. If the woman expresses discomfort or sets a boundary, it's important to respect it and not push for anything beyond that. It's also important to check in with her periodically to ensure that the boundaries are still being respected and to make any necessary adjustments.

Remember that every woman is unique and may have different preferences and expectations. By being respectful, communicative, and patient, you can build a strong foundation for a fulfilling relationship.

26

RETURNING TO THE LAND AND LIVING AS OUR ANCESTRAL Biblical FORE-PARENTS ONCE DID

Living Self-Sufficiently

L iving self-sufficiently and in a health-conscious way can certainly be valuable goals for individuals and families, and some people may find inspiration in the lifestyle practices of their ancestral foreparents. However, it's important to recognize that the world we live in today is vastly different from the world of our Biblical ancestors.

For example, our ancestors did not have access to modern medicine or the technology and infrastructure that enables us to live in large cities and travel great distances. They also had to contend with different environmental conditions and cultural practices that may not be applicable or desirable for us today.

Furthermore, the Bible is a complex and diverse text that has been interpreted and applied in a variety of ways throughout history. While there may be valuable lessons and principles to be gleaned from the Bible, it's important to engage with it critically and thoughtfully, recognizing its historical and cultural contexts and the limitations of our understanding.

Ultimately, the decision to live in a self-sufficient and health-conscious way is a personal one, with many paths and approaches that can lead to a fulfilling and balanced life. It's important to be mindful of the complexities and challenges involved and to seek out resources and support as needed.

It is not appropriate or ethical to make a blanket statement that returning to the land and living as our Hebraic foreparents did would be a wise decision for polygynous families. It is important to consider each family's unique circumstances, needs, and values, and to make decisions that prioritize the well-being and agency of all family members involved.

Polygyny, which involves a man having multiple wives, is a complex and often controversial practice that is not widely accepted or practiced in many societies today. While it is mentioned in the Bible, it is important to recognize the historical and cultural contexts in which it was practiced and how it may have been influenced by patriarchy and power dynamics.

Furthermore, returning to the land and living in a self-sufficient way can involve a great deal of work and effort, and it may not be feasible or desirable for all families. It is important to consider factors such as access to resources, physical abilities, and personal preferences when making decisions about lifestyle choices.

Ultimately, it is up to each individual and family to make informed and thoughtful decisions about how to live their lives and to prioritize the well-being and agency of all family members involved. It is important to approach these decisions with openness, curiosity, and a willingness to learn and adapt over time.

While it is understandable to be concerned about the potential for societal collapse or other disruptions, it is important to approach such decisions with careful consideration and a realistic understanding of the risks and challenges involved.

Relocating to a naturally resource-rich land can certainly have benefits in terms of self-sufficiency and resilience, but it also requires careful planning and preparation. Factors such as access to water, arable land, and other resources should be carefully evaluated, as well as the potential risks from natural disasters, political instability, and other factors.

It is also important to consider the impact of such a decision on your family members, including their emotional well-being, social connections, and access to education and other resources. Relocating to a remote or isolated area can have significant challenges in terms of social isolation and limited access to healthcare and other services.

Ultimately, the decision to relocate to a resource-rich land should be based on a careful evaluation of the risks and benefits involved, as well as a realistic assessment of your family's unique circumstances and needs. It is important to approach such decisions with an open mind and a willingness to adapt and adjust over time, as the situation may evolve and change.

Relocating to a resource-rich land and living as our Biblical ancestors did can be a complex and challenging endeavor, but it is not impossible. Here are some general steps that you may find helpful:

1. **Research and evaluate potential locations:** Start by researching and evaluating potential locations that meet your criteria for a resource-rich land. Look for areas with access to water, fertile soil, and other necessary resources. Consider factors such as climate, topography, and potential risks from natural disasters or political instability.

2. **Develop a plan for sustainable living:** Living sustainably on the land involves developing a plan for how to provide for your basic needs, such as food, water, shelter, and energy. Consider factors such as permaculture, composting, rainwater harvesting, solar power, and other sustainable practices.

3. **Acquire necessary skills and knowledge:** Living on land requires a wide range of skills and knowledge, including farming, animal husbandry, construction, and wilderness survival. Consider taking courses, workshops, or apprenticeships to develop these skills.

4. **Build a community:** Living on the land can be challenging, and it is important to build a community of like-minded individuals who can provide support, assistance, and companionship. Consider joining or forming an intentional community, or connecting with other individuals who share your goals.

5. **Adapt and adjust over time:** Living on the land can be a dynamic and ever-evolving process. Be prepared to adapt and adjust your plans and practices as needed, and be open to learning from your experiences and those of others.

It's important to approach this kind of lifestyle change with realistic expectations and a willingness to adapt and adjust over time. While living on the land can be incredibly rewarding, it is also challenging and requires a significant investment of time, energy, and resources.

Researching and evaluating potential locations is an important first step in relocating to a resource-rich land. Here are some factors to consider when evaluating potential locations:

• **Access to water:** Water is essential for human survival and agriculture, so it is important to look for locations with access to a reliable source of water, such as a river, stream, lake, or groundwater.

- **Fertile soil:** Fertile soil is necessary for growing crops and raising livestock, so it is important to look for locations with soil that is suitable for agriculture.

- **Climate:** Climate can have a significant impact on the ability to grow crops and raise livestock, so it is important to consider factors such as temperature, rainfall, and seasonal variations.

- **Topography:** The topography of the land can affect the ability to cultivate crops and raise livestock, so it is important to consider factors such as slope, elevation, and drainage.

- **Natural disasters:** Some locations may be more prone to natural disasters such as floods, earthquakes, tornadoes, hurricanes, or wildfires. It is important to evaluate the risks associated with potential natural disasters and take steps to mitigate those risks.

- **Political stability:** Political stability is important for ensuring access to resources and maintaining a safe living environment. It is important to research the political situation in the area you are considering and consider any potential risks associated with political instability.

By carefully evaluating potential locations based on these factors, you can identify areas that are likely to provide the necessary resources and support for a sustainable lifestyle.

Living sustainably on the land will also require developing a plan for meeting your basic needs. Here are some sustainable practices to consider:

- **Permaculture:** Permaculture is a design system that emphasizes working with natural processes to create sustainable agricultural systems. By mimicking natural ecosystems, permaculture systems can be highly productive and resilient.

- **Composting:** Composting is a natural process of breaking down organic materials into rich soil. By composting food waste, yard waste, and other organic materials, you can produce nutrient-rich soil for growing crops.

- **Rainwater harvesting:** Collecting and storing rainwater can provide a reliable source of water for irrigation and other uses. Rainwater harvesting systems can range from simple barrels to more elaborate cisterns and storage tanks.

- **Solar power:** Solar power can provide a reliable source of electricity for lighting, heating, and other uses. Solar panels can be installed on rooftops or mounted on poles to capture energy from the sun.

- **Natural building:** Natural building techniques use locally available materials to construct durable and sustainable buildings. Materials such as adobe, straw bales, and timber can be used to construct buildings that are energy-efficient and well-suited to the local climate.

By incorporating these and other sustainable practices into your plan for living on the land, you can create a self-sufficient and resilient lifestyle that is less dependent on outside resources. However, it is important to note that living sustainably on the land requires a significant investment of time, energy, and resources, and it may take time to fully develop a self-sufficient system.

Developing a wide range of skills and knowledge is essential for living on the land. Here are some ways to acquire the necessary skills:

- **Courses and workshops:** Many organizations offer courses and workshops on sustainable living, farming, animal husbandry, construction, and wilderness survival. Attending these classes can be a great way to learn from experienced instructors and connect with other like-minded individuals.

- **Apprenticeships:** Apprenticeships provide an opportunity to learn directly from experienced practitioners in a hands-on setting. By working alongside a skilled farmer, builder, or animal caretaker, you can gain practical experience and learn valuable skills.

- **Homesteading books and online resources:** There are many books and online resources available that provide information on sustainable living, farming, animal husbandry, and construction. These resources can be a great way to learn the basics and get ideas for how to apply these practices in your own life.

- **Community networks:** Joining a local homesteading or sustainable living community can provide opportunities to learn from others who are already living on the land. Community members can share information and resources, offer advice and support, and provide opportunities for hands-on learning.

By taking advantage of these and other resources, you can develop the skills and knowledge needed to live sustainably on the land. It is important to remember that developing these skills takes time and effort, but the rewards of self-sufficiency and a deeper connection with the natural world can be well worth it.

Building a community of like-minded individuals is essential for living on the land. Here are some ways to connect with others:

- **Join an intentional community:** Intentional communities are groups of people who live together and share resources, often to live sustainably and foster a sense of community. Joining an intentional community can provide a built-in support system and opportunities for learning and collaboration.

- **Attend events and gatherings:** Attending events such as home-steading fairs, sustainable living festivals, and other gatherings can provide opportunities to connect with others who share your interests and goals.

- **Online groups and forums:** There are many online groups and forums dedicated to sustainable living, homesteading, and related topics. Joining these groups can provide opportunities to connect with others, ask questions, and share resources.

- **Local networks:** Building relationships with local farmers, homesteaders, and other individuals who share your interests can provide opportunities for collaboration and support.

By building a community of like-minded individuals, you can share knowledge, resources, and support as you work to live sustainably on the land. Whether you join an intentional community or simply connect with others in your local area, building relationships with others can help you overcome challenges and find greater fulfillment in your journey.

Living on the land requires flexibility and a willingness to adapt. Here are some more things to keep in mind as you plan to relocate your Divine Family Unit to the land you've chosen:

- **Be open to new ideas and approaches:** There is no one "right" way to live sustainably on the land. Be willing to explore different practices and techniques, and be open to learning from others.

- **Embrace trial and error:** Sustainable living involves a lot of trial and error. Be willing to experiment and try new things, and be prepared to learn from your mistakes.

- **Stay connected with your community:** Building relationships with other homesteaders and sustainable living practitioners can provide a valuable source of knowledge and support. Stay connected with your community and be willing to ask for help and advice when needed.

- **Stay informed:** Stay up-to-date on the latest developments in sustainable living, and be willing to incorporate new practices and technologies into your lifestyle as they become available.

By staying flexible and adaptable, you can continue to refine and improve your sustainable living practices over time. Remember that living on the land is a journey, not a destination, and that there is always more to learn and discover.

As the man and leader of your family, you would do well to keep in mind that relocating to the land and living holistically takes time and will not happen quickly. For example, attempting to relocate your entire family during an emergency where society essentially shuts down, similar to what took place during the Covid-19 pandemic, would be extremely difficult due to the many factors involved with acquiring land.

Packing up an entire home and then navigating your family to the new property during a societal emergency will not be easy either. The majority of this modern-day society has become accustomed to thinking within a "microwave mentality" where everything happens immediately, almost at the push of a button, however, there are still many elements of life that are "non-microwavable", and acquiring land that you will relocate your family to is one of them.

The points being made here are not to fear-monger but are instead a multi-faceted attempt to help you realize the nuanced aspects of identifying good, naturally resource-rich land, communicating with real estate agents and property sellers, packing up your home, and relocating your family, especially at the last minute or during an emergency.

You will also need to take into account that you will have to learn the layout of the land you purchase and familiarize yourself with it. The time of the year you relocate matters also, especially if you have plans on growing crops and building structures on your property.

There are many hurdles that you will have to overcome along your journey, with your mental fortitude being tested every single step of the way, so keep in mind that your family is watching how you handle adversity.

Ensuring that you conduct the proper due diligence before embarking upon your journey will be helpful, but will not be fail-safe. Maintaining an active prayer life, and consulting with individuals who have experience with identifying a suitable property and relocating their family and possessions is highly recommended.

Living as our Biblical ancestors and ancestresses did can be rewarding and well worth the effort, as long as you stay committed to the process and don't give up. If you expect to receive the blessings of Jeremiah 29:6-7, you will have to learn how to pray for the peace and prosperity of the place you find yourself and your family located within.

27

PLANNING ACTIVITIES AND TRAVELING WITH YOUR GROWING FAMILY

Family Travels & Activities

P lanning activities and traveling with your family can be a wonderful way to create lasting memories and strengthen bonds between family members. Embarking on a fun journey as a Divine Family Unit can present its unique challenges. In this chapter, we will discuss the importance of togetherness, trip logistics, and maintaining harmony amongst all members of your Divine Family Unit.

When we plan activities and travel with our family we create opportunities to spend quality time together. With busy schedules and different priorities, it can be challenging to find time to connect with your family members. Planning activities and traveling together creates a shared experience that allows everyone to bond and make memories.

Shared experiences create a sense of belonging and unity. You should be well aware by now that expanding your family will be no easy task. When we add to our family, some members can feel as though they no longer belong, or that they aren't appreciated any longer. Planning activities and traveling with your family creates a common goal and a shared experience that everyone can relate to.

These shared experiences can create lasting memories and stories that can be passed down through generations. Sharing these types of experiences also reassure each member of the family that they hold a valued role within the family structure.

Traveling and trying new activities exposes your family to different cultures, traditions, and experiences. This exposure broadens your family's perspectives and encourages curiosity and learning. Exposure to new things helps develop open-mindedness, tolerance, and empathy.

Open-mindedness, tolerance, and empathy are important qualities that each member of a polygynous family must have. Polygynous families are unique and complex family structures, and all family members need to have these qualities to foster positive relationships and create a harmonious family environment.

Open-mindedness is crucial in a polygynous family as it allows each member to be receptive to new ideas, perspectives, and ways of doing things. Open-mindedness enables family members to appreciate and respect each other's differences, which is essential for maintaining healthy relationships. It also allows for the exploration of new experiences and opportunities, which can enrich the family's dynamic.

Tolerance is another important quality in an expanding family. Each member has a unique personality and interests in a Divine Family Unit. Tolerance allows each member to acknowledge and accept these differences without judgment, criticism, or rejection. Tolerance also creates a non-judgmental environment that fosters trust, respect, and mutual understanding, which are essential for creating positive relationships in a polygynous family.

Empathy is also an essential element within a polygynous family as it allows family members to understand and connect with each other's feelings and emotions. Empathy enables family members to put themselves in each other's shoes and understand how their actions and words affect others. Creating a safe space for communication and allowing family members to express themselves honestly and openly, is vital in maintaining positive relationships.

Cultivating these qualities will enable family members to appreciate and respect each other's differences, create a non-judgmental environment, and foster mutual understanding and trust, which are essential for maintaining positive relationships in a Divine Family Unit.

Getting out and traveling with your family can be a lot of fun and provide an opportunity for adventure. It's a chance to step outside your comfort zone and try new things. These fun and exciting experiences can create a sense of joy and happiness that is contagious and can strengthen family bonds.

On-lookers will be curious, and amazed at the sight of your family as you travel, so expect them to inquire about the structure of your Divine Family Unit. Making the members of your family aware of this in advance will prepare them and keep everyone's energy vibrating at a high frequency.

Communication between family members is a major key to having a fun-filled excursion. When we plan activities and travel with our family, we are provided a chance for open communication, allowing for a deeper understanding of one another. It provides a safe space to talk, share experiences, and bond over common interests.

One of the most exciting aspects of traveling with your family will be that of creating traditions. Taking your family on special outings creates an opportunity to establish traditions that can be passed down through generations. These traditions can be unique to your family and create a sense of identity and belonging. The experiences that are created become priceless memories with benefits that can enhance family relationships and create a sense of unity that can last a lifetime.

Here are some suggestions and ways you can make the most of your family travels and activities:

1. **Involve the whole family in planning:** Let everyone have a say in where you go and what you do. This will give everyone a sense of ownership and excitement about the trip.
2. **Create a travel bucket list:** Sit down as a family and make a list of all the places you want to visit and things you want to do together. This will help you prioritize your trips and ensure everyone gets to experience something they want to do.
3. **Choose activities that everyone can enjoy:** Be mindful of the different ages and interests of your family members, and try to find activities that everyone can participate in and enjoy.
4. **Make time for downtime:** While it's important to fill your itinerary with fun activities, it's also important to have some downtime to relax and spend quality time together as a family.
5. **Take lots of photos:** Capture all the special moments and memories by taking lots of photos and creating a family photo album or scrapbook.

Involving the whole family in planning activities and trips is an excellent way to foster a sense of ownership and excitement within a polygynous family. When everyone has a say in where to go and what to do, it creates a sense of teamwork, unity, and shared responsibility. It also ensures that each family member's interests and preferences are taken into account, which can help avoid conflicts and promote harmony.

In a polygynous family, involving everyone in the planning process can help create a sense of inclusiveness and equal participation. It allows each family member to have a voice and a role in making decisions that affect the family as a whole. It also provides an opportunity for family members to share their ideas and opinions, which can help strengthen communication and understanding.

Additionally, involving everyone in planning activities and trips can increase the excitement and anticipation leading up to the trip. Each family member can look forward to the trip with enthusiasm, knowing that they had a part in planning it. This excitement can create a sense of togetherness and shared experience that can help foster positive relationships within a polygynous family.

Creating a travel bucket list is an excellent idea for your Divine Family Unit to prioritize their trips and ensure that everyone gets to experience something they want to do. A travel bucket list is a list of places or experiences that a family wants to visit or have during their travels.

As a polygynous family, sitting down together and creating a travel bucket list is an opportunity to discuss everyone's travel goals, preferences, and expectations. This discussion can help create a sense of inclusiveness and equal participation, where each family member's interests and preferences are taken into account. It can also help avoid conflicts and promote harmony by identifying and addressing potential disagreements before they arise.

Creating a travel bucket list can also help prioritize family trips by identifying the places or experiences that are most important to each family member. This prioritization ensures that each family member gets to experience something they want to do, which can foster positive relationships within the family.

Moreover, creating a travel bucket list can help the family plan and save for future trips. The list can serve as a guide for the family's travel goals and help them budget and plan for each trip accordingly. It can also increase excitement and anticipation leading up to the trip, as the family members look forward to crossing off items on their bucket lists.

Implementing a travel bucket list into your outing is an excellent way for a polygynous family to prioritize their trips and ensure that everyone gets to experience something they want to do. It fosters inclusiveness, equal participation, and positive relationships within the family. It also helps the family plan and budget for future trips and increases excitement and anticipation leading up to each trip.

Incorporating tips like these into your family activities and travels will assist you with creating lifelong memories and a strong bond that will last a lifetime. When considering the legacy you seek to leave, these are important objectives that must be met.

Choosing activities that everyone can enjoy is essential in a polygynous family to show that each member is considered and valued. Being mindful of the different ages and interests of family members is crucial in finding activities that everyone can participate in and enjoy.

In a polygynous family, there may be significant age differences between family members, which means finding activities that cater to each age group can be challenging. It is essential to choose activities that cater to the interests and abilities of each family member to ensure that everyone feels included and valued. For instance, if some family members enjoy hiking, while others prefer water activities, planning a trip that includes both hiking and water activities can cater to everyone's interests and ensure that no one feels left out.

Moreover, when planning activities in a polygynous family, it is essential to ensure that no one feels excluded due to cultural, religious, or personal beliefs. In such cases, it may be necessary to research the destination and activities to ensure they align with the family's beliefs and values. As a Hebraic-thinking family, each member should be in alignment with the core values provided to us in Torah.

By choosing activities that cater to everyone's interests and abilities, the polygynous family can create a positive and inclusive environment. It can also help build relationships within the family by creating shared experiences and memories that everyone can cherish.

One of our goals as the head of our family should be to illustrate how important each member is considered and valued. It is necessary to be mindful of the different ages and interests of family members and choose activities that cater to them. By doing so, the family can create a positive and inclusive environment, build relationships, and create shared experiences and memories that everyone can cherish.

One of the most overlooked aspects of travel with family is downtime. Making time for downtime is crucial in a polygynous family, just as it is in any family structure. While it is tempting to fill every moment of the itinerary with activities, it is essential to have some downtime to relax and spend quality time together as a family.

Downtime can take many forms, such as enjoying a picnic in the park, reading a book, or simply having a conversation. Downtime allows family members to decompress from the excitement of the trip, recharge, and connect. It also provides an opportunity for family members to engage in activities they enjoy individually or as a smaller group within the larger family structure.

In the context of a polygynous family, making time for downtime can be particularly important. The family structure can involve multiple households with different schedules, routines, and needs. Scheduling downtime into the trip itinerary can help ensure that everyone has a chance to rest, recharge, and spend quality time together, regardless of their living arrangements when the trip has concluded and everyone returns home.

Furthermore, downtime can also provide an opportunity for family members to discuss and process the activities they have participated in and the experiences they have had. This can be particularly important in a polygynous family, where communication and understanding between family members can sometimes be challenging due to age differences, and roles within the family.

While promoting harmonious interactions among family members, fostering communication and understanding within the family will be a constant focus of yours. Over time, this can take its toll on you. Taking some downtime for yourself as the head of the family is just as important as scheduling downtime for the family as a whole.

As the head of a polygynous family, you will likely be responsible for coordinating and planning the family's activities and travels. This can be a demanding and stressful role, and it is essential to take some time to recharge and rejuvenate yourself.

Taking some time for yourself can involve engaging in activities that you enjoy independently, such as reading a book, going for a walk, or practicing meditation. It can also involve taking a break from the responsibilities of family planning and delegating some of those tasks to other family members.

It is important to remember that taking time for yourself does not make you a less devoted or responsible head of the family. On the contrary, it can help you be a better leader by reducing stress, improving your mental health and well-being, and allowing you to approach family planning and decision-making with renewed energy and focus.

Furthermore, modeling the importance of self-care to your family can also help encourage them to prioritize their well-being and self-care. This can help foster a culture of mutual support and care within your Divine Family Unit.

While engaging in all of the fun of journeying together you must remember to document your adventure!

Taking lots of photos on your adventure is a wonderful way to capture all the special moments and memories you create together. By documenting your travels and experiences through photographs, you can create a family photo album or scrapbook that you can all cherish for years to come.

Photographs can serve as a reminder of all the adventures you have shared and can help you relive those experiences even after they have passed. They can also be a way to bond as a family by sharing stories and reminiscing about the good times you've had.

In addition to traditional photo albums and scrapbooks, there are also many digital options for storing and sharing your family photos. You can create shared albums on platforms like Google Photos or iCloud, or even create a private family blog or website where you can share your photos and stories.

Creating a private family blog or website will require extra time and maintenance, but is a great way to get the younger members of the family involved with the responsibilities of upkeeping the family's media.

By taking lots of photos and creating a shared photo album or scrapbook, you are not only preserving your family's memories but also building a legacy that can be passed down to future generations. It is a wonderful way to create a sense of family history and tradition and to reinforce the bonds between family members.

Strengthening Bonds & Enjoying The Experience

As mentioned earlier in this chapter, strengthening family bonds is of the utmost importance. Traveling to vacation destinations with your family isn't the only way to strengthen bonds with them. Planning activities like outings to the park, sports training, and even grocery shopping are just as important and provide numerous benefits for both parents and children.

Strengthening family bonds doesn't always require going on extravagant trips or vacations. Simple activities and outings can be just as effective in building strong relationships and creating lasting memories.

Activities like going to the park or engaging in sports training together can be a great way to spend quality time as a family. It allows parents and children to engage in physical activity together, which has numerous health benefits. It also provides an opportunity to teach important life skills like teamwork, sportsmanship, and perseverance.

Engaging in a sport like martial arts as a family can be a great way to bond and work towards shared goals. Martial arts can teach valuable life skills like discipline, respect, and perseverance while also improving physical fitness and coordination.

Training together as a family can be a fun and rewarding experience. It provides an opportunity to support and encourage each other through the challenges of training, while also strengthening the bond between family members. Additionally, it can be a great way to build self-confidence and improve communication skills.

Working towards shared goals, such as earning a new belt or mastering a new technique, can be an exciting and rewarding experience for the whole family. It creates a sense of unity and purpose that can carry over into other aspects of family life.

Martial arts training also provides a healthy outlet for stress and can help promote mental wellness. It can be a great way to unwind and recharge after a long day, while also fostering a sense of mindfulness and self-awareness.

It's important to choose a martial arts style and training environment that is safe and suitable for all members of the family and to approach training with a positive and supportive attitude.

Even something as mundane as grocery shopping can be turned into a fun family outing. Involving children in the shopping process can teach them valuable lessons about budgeting, nutrition, and meal planning. It also provides an opportunity for parents and children to bond over shared interests and experiences.

While grocery shopping may not seem like the most exciting activity, it can be a valuable opportunity for families to bond and learn together.

Firstly, grocery shopping as a family can be a great way to teach children about healthy eating habits and nutrition. It provides an opportunity to discuss the importance of choosing whole foods and balanced meals and to involve children in the decision-making process of what foods to buy.

Secondly, grocery shopping can be a chance to practice life skills like budgeting and planning. Parents can involve children in creating a grocery list and sticking to a budget, teaching important money management skills in a practical setting.

Grocery shopping can also be a fun and interactive activity. Parents can involve children in the process of selecting and weighing produce, and older children can help with tasks like scanning items at the checkout. It provides an opportunity for quality family time and can create positive memories and experiences.

Finally, grocery shopping as a family can also be a chance to support local businesses and agriculture. Visiting farmers' markets or local food co-ops can teach children about the importance of community and sustainability, while also promoting a sense of pride and connection to their local area. Supporting local businesses and growers also teaches your children the importance of cultivating their food, entrepreneurialism, and revenue stream generation.

The overall key to strengthening family bonds is to find activities that everyone can enjoy and participate in. It's important to listen to each other's interests and preferences and to make an effort to include everyone in the planning process. Keep in mind that everyone will not always agree with each other. Strengthening family bonds is also about the camaraderie that is established through the support of one another and a willingness to participate in activities that one wouldn't normally choose to engage in.

As the head of your family, it's extremely important to maintain harmony between family members as well.

By prioritizing family time and engaging in activities together, you can create a sense of belonging and connection that will endure for years to come. These activities don't have to be expensive or time-consuming – what's most important is the quality time spent together and the memories created along the way.

Creating Memories

In a polygynous family, participating in activities and traveling together can be an excellent way to create lasting memories and strengthen bonds between family members.

When multiple wives and their children come together for a trip or activity, they have the opportunity to bond, learn from each other, and create new shared experiences that will be remembered and cherished for years to come. These experiences also build trust amongst members which will be extremely valuable as the family continues growing.

These shared experiences can also help to foster a sense of unity and cohesion within the polygynous family. By participating in activities and traveling together, family members can learn more about each other's interests, passions, and perspectives, and develop a greater appreciation and understanding of each other.

Trust, respect, and a sense of camaraderie among family members can be especially important in a polygynous family where multiple wives and their children may live separately and not always interact regularly.

Furthermore, participating in activities and traveling together can provide a break from the routine of daily life, allowing family members to relax, have fun, and enjoy each other's company. This can be especially important for busy polygynous families, where schedules and responsibilities can often become overwhelming. Taking time to engage in activities and travel together can help to promote a healthy work-life balance and reduce stress levels, leading to happier, healthier family dynamics overall.

Experiencing New Things

When traveling to different parts of the world, families in a polygynous setting can learn about new cultures, traditions, and ways of life. They can try new foods, participate in local customs, and gain a deeper appreciation for the diversity of the world.

This can broaden their perspectives, enhance their understanding of the world, and promote empathy and understanding toward people from different backgrounds. Children, in particular, can benefit greatly from these experiences as they can foster their curiosity and creativity, and help them become more adaptable and open-minded individuals.

Participation in activities and travel will enhance communication skills among family members in a polygynous setting. When families engage in shared experiences, they have more opportunities to communicate and connect.

Family members can share their thoughts, feelings, and perspectives, and work through any disagreements or challenges that arise. These shared experiences can also help families develop stronger bonds, as they create a sense of togetherness and shared memories. As a result, communication skills will increase greatly and family members can learn to work together more effectively, leading to stronger relationships and a more cohesive Divine Family Unit.

Identifying ways to keep your activity and travel choices simple can be a great way to reduce stress and unwind from the daily routine. It's an opportunity to disconnect from technology and enjoy each other's company in a new and exciting environment.

Many times there is a stigma that just because you are establishing your expanded family you have to do the most elaborate and expensive things, and if you cannot do these things, then you shouldn't be engaging in polygyny. What we have to take into account here, is that one major reason an expanded family should be created is to stimulate the wealth-growing process of the family, and not constantly diminish the family's wealth by taking expensive trips all across the world.

If you, as the head of your family, don't keep your spending habits in check, as well as the spending habits of your wives, you will end up creating debt for yourselves that will keep you further from the financially liberating aspects of life that an expanded family is supposed to help you generate.

Planning activities and travel, when there are multiple adults and children involved, can sometimes become overwhelming. Therefore, keeping it simple and focusing on the quality of the time spent together can help reduce stress and promote relaxation.

Choosing activities and destinations that allow for unplugging from technology and enjoying each other's company can create a peaceful and enjoyable environment for everyone involved. It can also help to prioritize activities and choose ones that don't require too much planning or effort so that the focus can be on having fun and making memories.

To recap, here are a few reasons why it's important to plan activities and travel with your family:

1. **Strengthening bonds:** Participating in activities and traveling together can strengthen family bonds and create a sense of unity among family members. It's an opportunity for parents and children to spend quality time together and build meaningful relationships.
2. **Creating memories:** Participating in activities and traveling together can create memories that will last a lifetime. These shared experiences

can be talked about for years to come and bring the family closer together.

3. **Experiencing new things:** Activities and travel provide opportunities to experience new things and learn about different cultures. This exposure can broaden the horizons of family members and help them develop a more global perspective.

4. **Enhancing communication skills:** Participating in activities and travel can enhance communication skills among family members. The shared experiences can provide opportunities for parents and children to discuss their thoughts and feelings and work through any issues that may arise.

5. **Reducing stress:** Participating in activities and travel can be a great way to reduce stress and unwind from the daily routine. It's an opportunity to disconnect from technology and enjoy each other's company in a new and exciting environment.

By involving everyone in the planning process, creating a travel bucket list, choosing activities that cater to everyone's interests and ages, making time for downtime, and taking lots of photos, you can create shared experiences that will bring your family closer together.

These experiences can also provide opportunities to learn about different cultures, enhance communication skills, and reduce stress, leading to personal growth and development for each family member.

Personal growth and development are important for each family member in a polygynous family because it helps them to become better individuals, which in turn, contributes to the overall well-being of the family. When each family member is growing and developing, they become more confident, self-aware, and able to handle challenges more effectively.

This can lead to better communication, less conflict, and stronger relationships between family members. Additionally, personal growth and development can also lead to increased success in various areas of life, such as career and education, which can benefit the entire family.

By encouraging and supporting personal growth and development for each family member, a polygynous family can create a positive and supportive environment for everyone to thrive.

Expanding Our Thinking

A man without vision cannot see past his nose. Your family will always depend upon your ability to see the things that they don't want to see or are unable to see. Your ability to read between the lines is always going to play a vital role in how you guide your family.

As you lean on and depend on The Highest, your wives and children will likewise be depending on you.

To plan successful family activities and trips, you need to have a clear vision of what you want to achieve. Having a clear vision is crucial for planning successful family activities and trips in the context of a polygynous family. This includes deciding on the destination, activities, budget, and logistics. It can help ensure that everyone is on the same page and has a common goal in mind.

What is the purpose of the trip? Is it to relax and unwind, bond as a family, or explore a new culture or destination?

Where do you want to go? Consider factors such as the time of year, climate, and distance from home.

What do you want to do during the trip? Are there specific activities or attractions that you want to experience as a family?

What is your budget for the trip? This will help you determine what is feasible and help you plan accordingly.

How will you get to your destination? Will you need to book flights or accommodations? What other logistics will you need to consider, such as transportation and meals?

These are all important questions that must be answered, as well as aspects of your journey that need to be included within your vision if you are to have a successful family trip.

Cultivating and maintaining a heightened sense of mental fortitude is something that many men don't consider when seeking to expand their family. Planning activities and travel with a growing family can be challenging and stressful at times. It requires mental fortitude to stay patient, focused, organized, and calm in the face of unexpected obstacles or setbacks.

It is essential to have the resilience and determination to stay focused on the goals and overcome any challenges that may arise during the planning and execution of family activities and trips. This includes being able to adapt to unexpected changes and setbacks, such as flight cancellations, weather issues, or other unforeseen circumstances.

Additionally, having mental fortitude can help you maintain a positive attitude and approach to problem-solving, which can help reduce stress and anxiety for both you and your family members. Ultimately, mental fortitude is key to successfully navigating the ups and downs of family life and creating positive, memorable experiences for everyone involved.

Planning activities and traveling with a family, especially in a polygynous family, can be a complex and time-consuming process. It's essential to take into account the interests and needs of each family member and plan accordingly. You may need to coordinate with multiple spouses and children and make sure everyone is on the same page. It can be challenging, but with proper planning and communication, it can also be a rewarding and memorable experience for everyone involved.

The ability to exercise patience cannot be stated enough. Planning activities and traveling with a growing family require patience. You need to be patient with your children, your spouses, and yourself. It's important to take breaks, relax, and enjoy the experience, rather than rushing from one activity to the next.

Patience is a key factor in the success of planning activities and traveling with a polygynous family, just as much as it is in the successful planning of activities and traveling with a monogamous one. It's important to remember that everyone has different needs, wants, and preferences, and it may take time to accommodate them all. Additionally, unexpected delays and obstacles may occur during the trip, which requires patience to overcome.

By staying patient and calm, you can help keep the trip enjoyable and stress-free for everyone involved. Let's take a moment to review the aspects of expanding our thought process and thinking that will influence the best results for us before and while traveling with our expanded family:

1. **Vision:** To plan successful family activities and trips, you need to have a clear vision of what you want to achieve. This includes deciding on the destination, activities, budget, and logistics.
2. **Mental fortitude:** Planning activities and travel with a growing family can be challenging and stressful at times. It requires mental fortitude to stay focused, organized, and calm in the face of unexpected obstacles or setbacks.

3. **Preparation:** Planning activities and traveling with your family requires a lot of preparation. You need to research destinations, plan itineraries, book accommodations, and transportation, pack and organize belongings, and ensure everyone's needs are met.

4. **Patience:** Planning activities and travel with a growing family requires patience. You need to be patient with your children, your partner, and yourself. It's important to take breaks, relax, and enjoy the experience, rather than rushing from one activity to the next.

You are beginning to realize if you haven't already, that planning activities and traveling with your growing family requires vision, mental fortitude, and a lot of preparation. However, the benefits of creating lifelong memories and strengthening family bonds make it all worth it. Allow these factors to motivate and propel you forward when times seem to be getting a little tougher than usual.

Focus on yourself, and how you internally handle pressurized issues. When you are operating at your best, you give each member of your family permission to do the same. They will be looking at how you handle moments of pressure.

Your actions will leave a lasting mark on their memories, especially in how they recall them when the time comes in their lives to handle a pressure situation. Make sure that you are intentional in your responses and that you are aware of the fact that all eyes will be on you.

Research & Budgeting

Identifying the external pressures from others while growing your family is so important. When you think about how successful you've been in laying the foundation of your initial family, you have to kind of reverse-engineer what you did, and similarly establish your subsequent family.

Keeping your focus when spending money is a huge aspect of maintaining structure and financial discipline within your family. Don't allow your incoming or subsequent wife to throw you off by allowing her energy or perspective spending habits to alter how you've grown to operate your family before you married her.

The scriptures instruct us as Hebrew Israelites to not be a respecter of persons (Deuteronomy 1:17), and this is one of those occasions where you need to be sharp and stick to your guns if you have a wife who likes to spend money.

Making a travel budget before you embark on your journey would be wise for you to consider and implement. Sticking to your budget will keep those loose spending habits in check and assist you in making difficult decisions when emotions begin to take over due to compulsive buying disorder, also known as oniomania.

You don't want to overspend and create unnecessary stress. Teach your wives and children discipline when opportunities to spend arise.

Creating and sticking to a travel budget is an important aspect of planning activities and traveling with a polygynous family. This can help prevent overspending and financial stress, as well as teach important lessons in financial discipline to the wives and children in the family.

It is important to involve everyone in the budget planning process so that your family is aware of the financial limitations and can make informed decisions about how to spend money during the trip. This can also teach the value of money management and responsibility, which are important life skills for all family members. By prioritizing financial planning and discipline, the family can enjoy the travel experience without unnecessary stress or financial burden.

Researching your destination is of utmost importance. Do some research on your destination to find out about local customs, events, and attractions that are suitable for your family dynamic. This will help you plan your itinerary and make the most of your trip.

Understanding the complexities of your destination is crucial in the context of a polygynous family because it helps ensure that the travel experience is enjoyable for everyone involved. Different cultures and customs may have different expectations for social interactions, dress, and behavior, so it is essential to be aware of them beforehand.

This knowledge will also help you choose activities and destinations that are appropriate for your family's interests and ages. Furthermore, researching can help you avoid potential dangers or discomforts, such as extreme weather conditions or political unrest. Your goal to facilitate the proper research beforehand can help you plan and execute a safe and enjoyable trip for the whole family.

It's important to pack appropriately before embarking upon your family vacation. Make sure you pack for the weather and activities you have planned. Also, pack snacks and entertainment for your children to keep them occupied during the journey.

Make a list of essential items for each family member and ensure everyone packs their bag. Packing according to the weather and activities planned also includes taking into account any cultural considerations or dress codes.

Be sure to bring along any necessary medication and first aid supplies. For instance, If you will be traveling outside of the United States, you must bring all of your health necessities because there is no guarantee your prescribed medications will be on hand in the country you are traveling to.

Remember to pack plenty of snacks and entertainment options for the children to keep them occupied during travel time. You also want to consider packing some items that can make the trip more comfortable, such as pillows, blankets, or travel neck pillows.

Being flexible with your plans is a mindset you will need to have as well. Be prepared to adjust your plans if necessary. Don't let unexpected events ruin your trip, and be open to trying new things.

Making mental space for flexibility and adaptability to changes during your family vacation is important. It's essential to remember that things don't always go as planned, and unexpected events or circumstances may arise. Being open to adjusting your plans can help ensure that you have a more enjoyable and stress-free experience. It can also be an opportunity to try new things and make unexpected, unforgettable memories with your family.

It's important to have a backup plan and be open to changing your itinerary if necessary. This could be due to unexpected weather conditions, illness, or unforeseen events that may arise during the trip. Being flexible and adaptable can help reduce stress and ensure that everyone can still have a great time despite any changes to the original plan.

Finally, what's the point of a family journey if you don't Have fun? Remember, the most important thing is to have fun and enjoy each other's company. Don't get too caught up in the planning and logistics, and take time to relax and have fun with your family.

It's of the essence to remember that the purpose of a family vacation is to spend quality time together and create lasting memories. It's okay if things don't go according to plan or if there are hiccups along the way - what matters most is that you enjoy each other's company and have fun together.

So don't forget to let loose, be silly, and make the most of your time together as a family!

Let's take another look at the primary aspects of research and budgeting for your family excursion by reviewing the best practices listed below:

1. **Make a travel budget:** Plan a budget that works for your family and stick to it. You don't want to overspend and create unnecessary stress.
2. **Research your destination:** Do some research on your destination to find out about local customs, events, and attractions. This will help you plan your itinerary and make the most of your trip.
3. **Pack appropriately:** Make sure you pack for the weather and activities you have planned. Also, pack snacks and entertainment for your children to keep them occupied during the journey.
4. **Be flexible:** Be prepared to adjust your plans if necessary. Don't let unexpected events ruin your trip, and be open to trying new things.
5. **Have fun:** Remember, the most important thing is to have fun and enjoy each other's company. Don't get too caught up in the planning and logistics, and take time to relax and have fun with your family.

By following these tips, and allowing for occasional mistakes to be made along the way, you can plan enjoyable and memorable activities and travels with your growing family. The amount of joy you will personally benefit from as the head of your family will be invaluable. You will be seen as an indispensable leader to each member of your family. Your position as husband and dad will be cherished for generations to come.

Respect

Respect is crucial in any family dynamic, particularly in a polygynous family where there are multiple spouses and children. It's important to show respect and consideration for everyone's feelings, and values when planning activities and travel.

This may involve having open and honest communication with all members of the family, being flexible and accommodating, and making an effort to understand and appreciate each other's differences. By showing respect for everyone in the family, you can create a harmonious and enjoyable environment for all.

It's important to show respect for all spouses and children when planning activities and travel. When traveling it is easy to lose ourselves in the moment and forget the sensitivity that is required to maintain the highest levels of shalom and harmony within the expanded family dynamic.

Remember that traveling can be stressful for some family members and that everyone has different needs and preferences. By showing respect and sensitivity, you can help ensure that everyone feels comfortable and included in the activities and travel plans. This can go a long way toward maintaining a positive and harmonious family dynamic.

If you disrespect a family member, ask them to join you in a conversation where you can address your actions and apologize to them.

Addressing the situation directly and apologizing for any disrespectful behavior can help to repair the relationship and prevent future conflicts. It's important to take responsibility for your actions and make amends, while also being open to hearing the other person's perspective and feelings.

You should also make sure that each spouse and your children have opportunities for quality time together with you. This can involve planning separate activities or outings that are tailored to each family unit's interests and needs.

Not taking this step in the planning process can come across as disrespectful because it will appear as though you are implementing a "one size fits all" approach, and were inconsiderate of each member's unique needs as valued members of the family.

Going above and beyond in this area of thoughtful planning will yield a great feeling amongst the members of the family and will highlight that you are a caring and contemplative leader.

It's an investment in your family's well-being that can provide benefits for years to come.

In summary, planning activities and traveling with a growing family in the context of a polygynous marital structure requires effective communication, involvement of all spouses and their children, careful logistics planning, respect for cultural differences and personal preferences, and attention to quality time for each family unit.

The suggestions mentioned within this chapter are a lot to consider. Have confidence in yourself that you can pull this off. The deeper you involve yourself with this process, the more accustomed you will be to leading your family in a manner that is healthy, emotionally fulfilling, and all-out fun.

28

Conclusion

I n this exploration of the growing popularity of polygyny, it becomes evident that individuals are drawn to this ancient family structure as a means of reconnecting with ancestral traditions and embracing a simpler way of life. However, the challenge lies in reconciling these traditional practices with the realities of the modern world, where social media and detached lifestyles prevail.

While polygyny offers communal aspects and attracts attention, practitioners must navigate the challenges discreetly due to the potential for controversy and judgment. This is especially important in a society that has been influenced by the historical imposition of monogamy as a result of colonization.

The pursuit of validation within polygyny leads many individuals to seek guidance from their faith, ancestral wisdom, and elders. They strive to learn and adopt the most beneficial practices for their unique family dynamics privately and conscientiously. However, some individuals are enticed by the allure of popularity and leverage social media to gain validation and transmute the negative perceptions associated with polygyny.

Sharing intimate details of one's personal experiences within the lifestyle is not without its challenges, as it requires vulnerability and discernment. Those who prioritize popularity over the proper practice of polygyny often face adverse consequences for themselves and their families, leading to regret and condemnation of the entire familial structure.

To truly understand the psychology behind the decisions made in embracing a polygynous lifestyle, it is essential to acknowledge the complexity and diversity of motivations. Attempting to unravel every reason may prove overwhelming, but by recognizing the multifaceted nature of these decisions, we can gain insight into the diverse paths that lead individuals to choose polygyny as a way of life.

In the journey of expanding your family through polygyny, it is crucial to prioritize the well-being and happiness of your initial wife. Cultivating a harmonious family dynamic and fostering positive relationships between wives is vital for the overall success of the family.

Open and honest communication is the foundation of a healthy polygynous relationship. By expressing feelings, concerns, and expectations, all parties can understand each other's perspectives and find common ground. Trust and open communication are essential components that help prevent toxicity and unhealthy behaviors.

Recognizing the innate qualities of women, such as gentleness, calmness, assertiveness, and understanding, is important in maintaining a nurturing environment. Building trust and maintaining open lines of communication requires effort and commitment from all individuals involved.

It is crucial to address toxic or unhealthy behaviors, regardless of the relationship structure. Setting boundaries, seeking support, and prioritizing the well-being and safety of all individuals are necessary steps in maintaining a healthy family dynamic.

Acknowledging and respecting the individual needs, feelings, and contributions of each wife within the Divine Family Unit is crucial. Creating an environment where everyone feels valued and appreciated fosters appreciation and understanding.

During the initial stages of entering polygyny, it is important to address any emotional unease or vulnerability your wives may experience. Reassurance and reaffirmation of their significance in your life are crucial in building a strong foundation.

Creating a well-balanced and peaceful environment, characterized by harmony, can inspire spouses to bring out their best selves. However, it is important to recognize that individual experiences and personalities are shaped by various factors beyond just gender.

While it is valuable to seek guidance and learn from others' experiences, it is important to remember that each family's journey is unique. Effective communication, understanding, and shared goals are key to building a fulfilling and balanced relationship.

Encouraging sisterhood and bonding between wives can enhance the overall well-being of the family. Establishing a communication protocol and addressing misunderstandings with patience and understanding can strengthen harmony within the family.

Recognizing and validating each other's emotions fosters a nurturing and caring atmosphere. Fairness and equality among wives should be prioritized to avoid feelings of jealousy or resentment.

Adapting these principles to your specific circumstances, values, and beliefs while maintaining a strong commitment to open communication, respect, and understanding is key to building a successful polygynous family.

In conclusion, the journey of expanding your family in a polygynous arrangement can be smoother and more fulfilling when approached with kindness, empathy, and compassion. The foundation of a harmonious family dynamic lies in open and honest communication, which allows for understanding, common ground, and the prevention of toxic behaviors.

Recognizing and respecting the individual needs, feelings, and contributions of each wife within the Divine Family Unit is vital. It is crucial to address any signs of emotional unease and reassure both of your wives of their significance in your life as you navigate the new chapter. Expanding the family should be seen as adding and multiplying upon the existing foundation, rather than subtracting or dividing.

Creating a well-balanced and peaceful environment, characterized by mutual respect and open communication, inspires each spouse to bring out their best selves and contribute with love, attention, calmness, and serenity. It is essential to appreciate the unique qualities and strengths of each wife while acknowledging that experiences and personalities are shaped by various factors.

Encouraging a sense of sisterhood between wives fosters a supportive and nurturing environment. Activities, shared interests, and bonding opportunities contribute to stronger connections and the overall well-being of the family. Establishing a communication protocol between wives from the beginning helps to prevent misunderstandings and maintain harmony, even when expectations may differ.

Validating emotions and showcasing empathy and compassion are key elements in building and maintaining a healthy relationship. Fairness and equality among wives are essential in preventing jealousy or resentment. Establishing guidelines for time, resources, and decision-making processes while promoting inclusion within the decision-making process can help maintain balance.

If challenges arise, seeking professional guidance from a therapist or counselor experienced in polygynous relationships can provide valuable support and mediation during challenging times. Outstanding Personal Relationships, founded by Coach Nazir and his co-wives, Coaches Fatimah and Nyla, is a renowned resource for polygynous advice and counseling.

Ultimately, every relationship is unique, and it is important to adapt these principles to your specific circumstances, values, and beliefs. By committing to open communication, respect, and understanding, you can create a fulfilling and balanced polygynous family dynamic that supports the growth and happiness of all its members.

I pray that you are blessed with the wisdom and discernment needed to navigate the nuances of an expanded family. May your homes be enriched. May your wives be happy. May your children grow in righteousness. May your Divine Family Unit thrive, and be a shining light to the rest of the world.

-True Ju

References

In this section, you will be able to locate all of the Scriptural references found within the pages of this book. Being able to easily identify and refer to them will assist you in your studies. Each chapter or sub-chapter that contains Scriptural passages will be noted in this section as well.

RECOGNIZING POLYGYNY IN THE SCRIPTURES

1. b - Polygyny: A Cultural Norm Throughout Biblical History

- Genesis 4:19
- Deuteronomy 21:15-17
- Genesis 2:24
- 1 Timothy 3:2
- Jeremiah 31:31-33
- 1 Kings 11:3
- Deuteronomy 7:3-4
- Deuteronomy 21:15-17
- Matthew 19:5

ABRAHAM AND HIS THREE WIVES

1. **a - Abraham And His Three Wives**

- Genesis 11:29
- Genesis 20:1-14
- Genesis 21:1-2
- Genesis 16
- Genesis 25:1-2

THE STORY OF JACOB AND HIS FOUR WIVES

1. **a - Jacob And His Service For His Uncle Laban**

- Genesis 32:28

THE STORY OF SOLOMON AND HIS MANY WIVES AND CONCUBINES

1. **b - Solomon's Reign and His Many Wives and Concubines**

- Deuteronomy 7:3-4
- Deuteronomy 17:17
- 2 Samuel 12:8

THE STORY OF GIDEON AND HIS MANY WIVES

- Judges 6-8

THE STORY OF ABIJAH AND HIS FOURTEEN WIVES

1. a - Who Was Abijah?

- 2 Chronicles 13:21

THE STORY OF ELKANAH AND HIS MANY WIVES

1. a - Who Was Elkanah?

- 1 Samuel 1-2

1. c - Who Was Hannah?

- 1 Samuel 2:1-10

THE STORY OF HAMASHIACH'S PARABLE OF THE WISE AND FOOLISH VIRGINS

1. a - One Parable That *Is Not* What It Seems At First Glance

- Matthew 25:1-13

1. b - A Misunderstood Law That Must Be Clarified

- Matthew 19:9

THE STORY OF MOSES AND HIS TWO WIVES

1. d - Who Was Zipporah?

- Exodus 18

1. e - Moses' Second Wife Was An Ethiopian Woman?

- Numbers 12:1

LEARNING HOW TO BE SUBMISSIVE AND NURTURING TO YOUR HUSBAND

- Ephesians 5:22-24
- Colossians 3:18-19
- Ephesians 5:33
- Ephesians 5:21

- Ephesians 5:25-28
- Genesis 2:18
- Philippians 2:3-4
- Proverbs 15:1
- Proverbs 15:33
- Colossians 3:23-24
- 1 Corinthians 7:3-5
- 1 Peter 3:7

HOW TO RECOGNIZE IF YOUR WIFE IS DEPRESSED OR FEELING LEFT OUT

1. b - Feelings Of Depression Are To Be Expected

- Proverbs 16:1-3

RETURNING TO THE LAND AND LIVING AS OUR ANCESTRAL BIBLICAL FORE-PARENTS ONCE DID

1. a - Living Self-Sufficiently

- Jeremiah 29:6-7

PLANNING ACTIVITIES AND TRAVELING WITH YOUR GROWING FAMILY

1. f - Research & Budgeting

- Deuteronomy 1:17

About the Author

TRUE JU -

Husband, Father, Spiritual Ambassador, Spiritual Counselor, Author, Motivational Speaker, Self-help Practitioner, Self-development Coach, Healer, Music Therapy Physician, Life Coach, and Survivor.

True Ju has expanded into all of the vocations mentioned above, and then some. He has worked hard in humility his entire life, striving to be the best person he can be at all times, despite the cards he was dealt. For over two decades, he has used his voice and gifts of healing to inspire and motivate people from all over the world to be their best selves.

As a direct result of his connection to the Divine since birth, True Ju has been blessed with the guidance to navigate through the toxicity and heartache he experienced in his early childhood and teenage years. He is now in a position to assist others in navigating through their own lives to find peace, balance, and harmony within.

True Ju is the self-published author of the 2022 international bestseller From Clutter To Cleanliness: The Renewal Of A Mind - A Success Story, as well as the founder and owner of one of the most successful audio and video distribution platforms in the world, catering to independent recording artists worldwide. He recently released his new book The Divine Family: A True Journey Into Biblical Polygyny and also coined the term "Divine Family Unit". He is the head of his own expanded family and enjoys the successes and challenges that arise from living within that biblically-based dynamic.

Here to make an effectual change on this planet, True Ju travels where others will not, helping and assisting those who are often disregarded, sharing the light of love and joy with whomever he meets.

True Ju is a Spiritual counselor and mentor, seeking to help others identify the Light, Love, and Gratitude they carry within themselves.

You can connect with me on:

- https://trueju.org
- https://twitter.com/trueju365
- https://www.youtube.com/channel/UCePl1Dlf4fqLhWEaYbFlwLQ

Subscribe to my newsletter:

- https://trueju.org/contact

Also by True Ju

From Clutter To Cleanliness: The Renewal Of A Mind – A Success Story is a book about accountability and taking charge of our lives once we have the ability and recognition to do so. This book is about healing and gratitude. This book is about being able to take what's happened throughout your life on the proverbial chin and continue fighting another day. This book is a reminder to be thankful in all aspects of life, enjoying the **Divine Refinement Process** as much as humanly possible.

True Ju has taken great lengths in ensuring that the motivational message within these pages is clear: there are no coincidences, and everything happens for a reason.

After reading this self-help book on healing and personal growth, you will feel relieved and grateful to have lived your unique experience and will have a better idea of why you should share your testimony, and how to share your testimony, with the world.

From Clutter To Cleanliness: The Renewal Of A Mind – A Success Story is packed with rich anecdotes as well as methods to help you overcome anxiety and speak life to yourself. No longer will you have to live with the excuse of "not knowing the way" and can finally propel yourself forward into the great destiny you were always meant to live.

Everyone has a story; it's just that everyone doesn't feel like their story is worthy enough to be shared. *From Clutter To Cleanliness: The Renewal Of A Mind – A Success Story* will gift you the life-changing methods that will free your mind and body from the debilitating conditions holding you back, which have kept your spirit from recognizing and claiming the greatness within.

From Clutter To Cleanliness: The Renewal Of A Mind – A Success Story

https://trueju.org/product/the-renewal-of-a-mind-pdf

"Everyone has a story; it's just that everyone doesn't feel like their story is worthy enough to be shared."